One Piece of the Puzzle Collection

What is the "One Piece of the Puzzle Collection?"

I used to enjoy putting puzzles together as a kid; usually it was a five hundred piece puzzle that we worked on together as a family. Every puzzle piece has their place on this puzzle, and when we examine a single puzzle piece alone by itself we don't really see that they are much different than all the other center puzzle pieces; all pretty much the same shape, but with different colors. So for this puzzle to have order, every piece of the puzzle had to be involved in the picture. In many ways you and I are just one piece of this grand puzzle made up of over seven billion puzzle pieces, and each piece of this great puzzle has an important place within this world created by God. Each person in this puzzle is so important to God, that He sacrificed His only son to die for each one of us on the cross, a death that now allows both you and me a chance to begin a new life freed of the burdens of our own sins. And with our new freedom in following Christ we are now better able to proclaim the Lord's love for the world, a message that will help point others towards Jesus at the cross.

Each of the books that I am writing for this One Piece of the Puzzle Collection will hopefully help each reader to grow in their relationship with Jesus. I truly believe God will call those people who need to read the message within these books. God has pointed out many such books like this to me over the years, books that have helped me grow in my faith and understanding of our Lord. The Lord has placed it upon my heart to write these books for him. The process for writing each book has allowed me a chance for deepening my relationship with the Lord, a relationship that touches and moves my heart each day.

This first book of the One Piece of the Puzzle Collection is called: "Following Jesus on the Narrow Path to God," it is a book about the hard choices for following Jesus throughout our lifetimes; despite the busy nature of our lives and the many distractions the world often entices us with each day. God is calling every person in the world to come home to Him in heaven, but this pathway can only be found through Jesus at the cross on Calvary. It is a journey where we must decide who we want to follow in life. Who will you follow, Jesus or the world? One path leads to everlasting life, while the other path leads to death. Our Lord wishes for us to choose his narrow path for it will bring us home to him in heaven.

Our journey on this narrow path to God is not always going to be easy for us, but the path that you will be on with Christ will open your eyes to many wonderful graces from the Lord. If your path is easy right now, then you are not moving forward at all on this path. We need to remember everything that Jesus experienced while he walked this earth, he didn't have the comfort of riding in the cars that we drive today, or for hopping on a plane to get to the other side of his country, no he had to walk the many narrow rocky paths to get to the various towns and villages he visited. The Lord's last journey was the hardest one of them all, the narrow path leading up to Calvary, carrying the sins of the world on his back.

FOLLOWING JESUS ON THE NARROW PATH TO GOD

ROBERT VAIL

FOLLOWING JESUS ON THE NARROW PATH TO GOD

iUniverse books may be ordered through booksellers or by contacting:

iUniverse LLC
1663 Liberty Drive
Bloomington, IN 47403
www.iuniverse.com
1-800-Authors (1-800-288-4677)

ISBN: 978-1-4917-4564-9 (sc)
ISBN: 978-1-4917-4563-2 (e)

Library of Congress Control Number: 2014915828

Printed in the United States of America.

iUniverse rev. date: 09/09/2014

TABLE OF CONTENTS

PREFACE

I am a son of a farmer here in Illinois, I come from a large family, we each had our own chores to do around the farm and home, and we worked hard, and played hard as well. I enjoyed sports, but was never any good at them. I didn't really like school, learning the various subjects was hard for me; I had to study many hours to get decent grades. I bought my first used car at the age of sixteen, and by my senior year I was working at three jobs each day, plus doing my work at home.

One of the reasons I did not do well in sports was because of my neuromuscular disease, it was slowly taking away my muscle strength, and at six feet five inches the basketball coach would have liked me to be a better player, I could stand under the net and touch it with my fingers, but my legs were so weak I couldn't jump higher than an inch off the floor. It was during my first year at college that my disease began to accelerate in weakening my muscles, so much so I had to quit school because I could barely walk anymore. So, I came home to face my disease head on and try to get a better understanding of what was happening to my body. We travelled to the Mayo Clinic to look for those answers, so we found out that I had Charcot-Marie-Tooth disease, and a second neuropathy that was accelerating my disease. There was no cure for my Charcot-Marie-Tooth disease, but there were medicines that could stop this second neuropathy from weakening my body further. It was during this physical struggle that I developed a deeper relationship with our Lord Jesus Christ.

I received my Bachelor's Degree in Special Education at Illinois State University, Normal, Illinois, working with children with physical disabilities. I later completed course work for certification in Trainable Mental Handicap and Behavioral Disability as well. I was a special education teacher for twenty-six years, working with children who either had a physical disability, or a severe intellectual disability, or a combination of both types of disabilities.

My role as a special education teacher blessed me each day in the classroom, for I was given an opportunity for serving those special children that were given to the world and their parents by God. Each child for the most part will live out their lives each day with a pure soul, a child who was incapable of sinning or in hurting other people. I recognized that each child I served in the classroom whose sole role in the world was to point others towards God. Each child's passion for life always inspired me every day to work harder and to strive to be as close to Jesus as possible each moment of the day. I worked hard to bridge their two worlds together, meaning the "normal" kid's world and the "special" kid's world—my hope as a teacher was to see the other student's eyes opened up enough to truly witness the truth and gift of their lives for the world. I wanted these teenagers to see that those students who the world sees as being different were really just like any other teenager in the school—a teenager who wanted to be surrounded by their friends and to be able to enjoy all the many activities that any other teenager in the school experienced.

ACKNOWLEDGMENTS PAGE

I would like to dedicate this book to all those students I have worked with throughout my lifetime, for they are the Master Teachers who are teaching the people of the world how to truly live in God's world. These children were born into a world and circumstances that were not of their own choosing, these children have faced each day with courage as they struggled to learn and master many new educational concepts, but more importantly in mastering those basic life skills that are necessary for daily living in the community. These most special individuals have always worked hard each day in doing the will of others:

1. Their Lord's will
2. Their parent's will
3. Their sibling's will
4. Their grandparent's will
5. Their teacher's will
6. Their assistant's will
7. Their caregiver's will

We have so much to learn from these special gifts from heaven. Each child I have found are naturally pure souls living amongst the world: who are always trusting, always loving, always courageous, always striving to overcome huge obstacles. These students were often isolated from others because of their intelligence levels, or by their lower communication abilities, and because they are so different from others. To me they were my heroes; I truly loved each one of these children because I recognized their purpose in God's world. I also developed a deep love and respect for each of the parents or care givers of these special gifts from heaven, and who each were especially chosen by God for this great task of caring for these children.

Note: I describe several of the students I have worked with over the years at various points within this book, and in order to protect their identity I gave them each a different name and I changed some of the specific details that reflected their daily life in this world. But, I can assure you that these children are very real and each child has had an impact on my life as their teacher, and their message of faith has taught me much about God's love for us all.

Special thanks to my wife Rowena who always inspires me every day by her own deep faith and love for Jesus. She keeps me anchored in my world, for she is the best friend I have ever had in my life.

I used the (NAB), New American Standard Bible as the source for all my scriptures within this book: Following Jesus on the Narrow Path to God. Much thanks to The Lockman Foundation! "Scripture taken from the New American Standard Bible®, Copyright © 1960, 1962, 1963, 1968, 1971, 1972, 1973, 1975, 1977, 1995 by The Lockman Foundation and used by permission."

INTRODUCTION

RUNNING THE TRAIL

I loved family picnics as a kid, it was a time where our families got together and shared a meal, it was a time for the grownups to get caught up in each one of their own sibling's lives, and for us kids it was a time to play with our cousins and siblings. Our family picnics usually occurred in the Princeton City Park on a Sunday after church, one of the family members would arrive early to claim an area with the right number of picnic tables for this occasion, and it had to be close to the bathrooms and also close to some playground equipment. It was a great way to spend an afternoon for a kid, lots of food, lots of iced tea or Kool-Aid to drink, and especially it gave us a chance to play with the cousins and siblings. This particular park had a series of narrow pathways that went up and down from the lower part of the park to the upper level of the park; its trails worked its way towards the back of the park where Lover's Leap was situated, a high bluff that overlooked the Bureau creek winding through the edge of the park, a beautiful sight to gaze at for a few moments of rest.

Running on the narrow path was an adventure for us kids, no longer needing the close eye of a parent, we could explore the paths as we saw fit. All of these pathways were narrow, with many turns, going up or down, surrounded by trees, bushes, many kinds of plants including some poison ivy. We would often have races going from one part of the park to another part of the park, so speed and skill was important for us kids to have for this race.

I was never very fast in running these narrow paths, but I did enjoy the adventure and excitement in exploring the park. Since, I was allergic to poison ivy I had to keep my eyes peeled for this plant so I wouldn't get poison ivy, but sometimes when I was going too fast down the path I would forget to look for these plants and I would end up getting poison ivy all over my arms and legs after a few days. So, it paid for me to go at a slower pace on the pathway, so I could see what plants I walked by on the trail. I also was a clumsy kid and tended to fall over things, so I had to always watch how I walked through an area, for I might trip on a tree root, or twist my ankle on a loose rock, or I might fall when stepping into a hole. It doesn't sound like running the pathways would be fun for me, but I enjoyed the adventure and the time shared with my cousins and siblings.

As a young man I loved being a part of nature, sitting deep within the woods, walking through nature parks, sitting by a lake or a river, just absorbing the beauty and peace found within nature. I loved driving across the country and visiting places of great beauty, from sitting by two oceans, from sitting on tops of several mountain ranges, from sitting on the edge of Grand Canyon, or a beautiful wheat or corn field. God has always touched my heart in these natural places. I also loved being around my family, especially my nieces and nephews who have always touched my heart by their unconditional love and energy. Today, I can no longer run these kinds of trails, nor can I easily get to these natural places in our country, nor can I no longer even walk across my own front lawn.

"Following Jesus on the Narrow Path to God," is partially a story of my life as I have gone down this narrow path, with all its turns, with all its dangers. This pathway has led me to Jesus and our Father in heaven, so I naturally want to use those things that God has used to shape my mind and beliefs:

1. Sacred scripture
2. Writings from the various Saints or other spiritual authors
3. The love of my family and friends
4. The Catholic Church, the Sacraments
5. Those moments from my journey where God gave me a special grace

"Following Jesus on the Narrow Path to God," is not really about me, but it is a book that is being written for you, so that you each can be encouraged in your own journey down this narrow pathway, following Christ to the cross. If we are going to finish our walk along this narrow path we have to keep our eyes on the path and be prepared for the dangers that touch our lives, we need to walk this journey with Jesus at our side, because Jesus is the path to God.

I want to close this section with a quote from one of my favorite books, "Hinds' Feet on High Places," by Hannah Hurnard, it is a book I read about every two years. In part this book is written because of this journey to the High Places, it is a journey we must begin today.

"But the High Places of victory and union with Christ cannot be reached by any mental reckoning of self to be dead to sin, or by seeking to devise some way or discipline by which the will can be crucified. The only way is by learning to accept, day by day, the actual conditions and tests permitted by God, by a continually repeated laying down of our will and acceptance of his as it is presented to us in the form of the people with whom we have to live and work, and in the things which happen to us." [1]

---

[1] *P.12, excerpt used from "Hinds' Feet on High Places," by Hannah Hurnard, Living Books, Tyndale House Publishers, London England, 1986, followed the guidelines set by Tyndale House Publishers (https://www.tatepublishing.com)*

CHAPTER 1

THE NARROW PATH

Have you ever looked at a geographical map of Israel? Jesus grew up in a very mountainous area that really had few roads for a person to travel on; the road or path was most likely a beaten track that people had trod on for many years. According to a map; Jesus lived about ninety miles away from Jerusalem, which means he may have travelled well over three thousand miles going to and from Nazareth and elsewhere in the thirty years he lived there with his family. You can add maybe another thousand miles during his ministry years. Israel didn't have the kinds of roads that we enjoy today, certainly not as wide, more like a wide path. Certainly the roads or paths going up into the many mountains were very rough and hard to navigate, often walking along the edge of a steep ravine.

Jesus did not have cars to zip him back and forth around his country; he most likely walked to all those places he visited during his lifetime. To go anywhere in Israel during that time period required lots of time and preparation: packing up food, water and clothes for the trip, food for the mule/camel, tents, tools, etc. If Jesus left on his own, he would still need to have carried food and water at least. The physical toll on the body would have increased especially during the warm season, requiring a greater supply of water and food.

I spent a day going through the Grand Canyon Park in Arizona one summer, it was fun watching the speed in which the tourists travelled through the park, driving into a pullout spot along the rim of the canyon, the family would pile out of the car and walk up to edge of the canyon and then take a picture, then they would jump back in the car and hurry down the road until the next turnout for a new sight, maybe only staying several minutes in each spot. Did each family member truly appreciate the great beauty of this park? I rather doubt it; because these tourists were moving too fast to notice the many beautiful facets of the canyon walls, or the fast moving river running through the canyon floor, nor could they see the colors change within the canyon as the sun moved overhead. I once spent several hours in one spot of the canyon just sitting and enjoying the beauty of the canyon and pondering the many wonders of God. When I think of the canyon today, I am thinking of the time I spent in that one beautiful spot where I was absorbed in the beauty and peace of this great treasure, and not from any of those other spots from the canyon where I had spent only a few minutes.

The pace of the people living during the time of Jesus was always tied to the pace in which one person was able to walk or travel down the pathway. Jesus surely had time to notice the beauty of the land as he walked, noticing how the mountains were shaped, or the beautiful valleys below, or the millions of flowers he passed while walking along these roads and pathways, or in seeing the sheep grazing on the hillsides, he most surely enjoyed the simple grace that the streams brought to a traveler as they passed them by, nor how could he not notice the beauty of the Sea of Galilee with its blue waters. We have scriptures where Jesus is gazing on Jerusalem from a distance, weeping over the fate of its future. Since travelling was so expensive and rare I think, Jesus must have especially enjoyed coming upon people and their caravans along the ways in which he travelled. Jesus had the time to take in each of their faces and probably greet each of the people along his journeys. But more importantly there was both time for walking in silence or it was a time for sharing of lives as they walked along the narrow roads or pathways, perhaps these were also the moments that Jesus talked about his heavenly Father to his Apostles and followers.

On a trip to Chicago, my wife Rowena and I passed thousands of cars and trucks, maybe passing over fifty thousand people. Did we truly see their faces and recognize them as human beings? Did we have the time to say hello and introduce ourselves? Did we have time to say a prayer for them? Probably not, because we were travelling too fast, we wanted to get to our motel within a set period of time. If we are going to follow Jesus today, we need to live at the kind of pace in which Jesus lived out his life. We need to see the world as Jesus saw the world; a world filled with immeasurable beauty as we continue to travel down that narrow path towards the cross, seeing both the beauty and the wonder of the world and the beauty and wonder of the world's many people.

"In the beginning, when God created the heavens and the earth, the earth was a formless wasteland, and darkness covered the abyss, while a mighty wind swept over the waters. Then God said, 'Let there be light,' and there was light. God saw how good the light was. God then separated the light from the darkness. God called the light 'day,' and the darkness he called 'night.' Thus evening came, and morning followed, the first day."

"Then God said, 'Let there be a dome in the middle of the waters, to separate one body of water from the other.' And so it happened: God made the dome, and it separated the water above the dome from the water below it. God called the dome 'the sky.' Evening came, and morning followed, the second day."

"Then God said, 'Let the water under the sky be gathered into a single basin, so that the dry land may appear.' And so it happened: the water under the sky was gathered into its basin, and the dry land appeared. God called the dry land 'the earth, and the basin of the water he called the sea.' God saw how good it was. Then God said, 'Let the earth bring forth vegetation: every kind of plant that bears seed and every kind of

*fruit tree on earth that bears fruit with its seed in it.'
And so it happened: the earth brought forth every kind
of plant that bears seed and every kind of fruit tree on
earth that bears fruit with its seed in it. God saw how
good it was. Evening came, and morning followed, the
third day."*

*"Then God said: 'Let there be lights in the dome of the
sky, to separate day from night. Let them mark the fixed
times, the days and the years, and serve as luminaries
in the dome of the sky, to shed light upon the earth.'
And so it happened: God made the two great lights,
the greater one to govern the day, and the lesser one to
govern the night; and he made the stars. God set them
in the dome of the sky, to shed light upon the earth, to
govern the day and the night, and to separate the light
from the darkness. God saw how good it was. Evening
came, and morning followed, the fourth day."*

*"Then God said, 'Let the water teem with an abundance
of living creatures, and on the earth let birds fly beneath
the dome of the sky.' And so it happened: God created the
great sea monsters and all kinds of swimming creatures
with which the water teems, and all kinds of winged
birds. God saw how good it was, and God blessed them,
saying, 'Be fertile, multiply, and fill the water of the
seas; and let the birds multiply on the earth.' Evening
came, and morning followed, the fifth day."*

*"Then God said, 'Let the earth bring forth all kinds
of living creatures: cattle, creeping things, and wild
animals of all kinds.' And so it happened: God made
all kinds of wild animals, all kinds of cattle, and all
kinds of creeping things of the earth. God saw how
good it was. Then God said: 'Let us make man in our
image, after our likeness. Let them have dominion over*

the fish of the sea, the birds of the air, and the cattle, and over all the wild animals and all the creatures that crawl on the ground.' God created man in his image; in the divine image he created him; male and female he created them. God blessed them, saying: 'Be fertile and multiply; fill the earth and subdue it. Have dominion over the fish of the sea, the birds of the air, and all the living things that move on the earth." God also said: 'See, I give you every seed-bearing plant all over the earth and every tree that has seed-bearing fruit on it to be your food; and to all the animals of the land, all the birds of the air, and all the living creatures that crawl on the ground, I give all the green plants for food.' And so it happened. God looked at everything he had made, and he found it very good. Evening came, and morning followed, the sixth day."

"Thus the heavens and the earth and all their array were completed. Since on the seventh day God was finished with the work he had been doing, he rested on the seventh day from all the work he had undertaken. So God blessed the seventh day and made it holy, because on it he rested from all the work he had done in creation."[2]

From the book of Genesis we can recognize that when God spoke, the world responded to those words:

1. The world needed light, light appeared.
2. The world needed darkness, darkness appeared.
3. The world needed a sky, the sky appeared.
4. The world needed water, water appeared.
5. The world needed land, every kind of land appeared.
6. The world needed vegetation, every kind of vegetation appeared.

---

[2]   *Gen.1:1-32 and Gen.2:1-3,NAB*

7. The world needed a night and a day, and the day and the night were separated by the sun, the moon and stars.
8. The world needed both land and water creatures, and every kind of animal and insects were formed.
9. The world needed a man made in the image of God, and man was formed and breathed upon.
10. When the work was done, God commanded that there be a day of rest.

I think we get the picture, God speaks and the action should now be completed through each man or woman; even our own birth in the world is a reaction to what God wanted for His world.

11. God speaks with Noah; Noah builds the ark and saves his family and the world.
12. God speaks to Abram; Abram leaves his home and moves his family a thousand miles away because God asked him to do this command.
13. God speaks with Moses on Mt. Sinai; Moses responds by going back to Egypt and forces the Pharaoh to free the Israel people who were enslaved for hundreds of years.
14. God spoke to prophets asking them to bring the people back to God; the prophets responded by going to these nations and proclaiming God's love for them and calling them to come home to Israel.
15. God sent his angel Michael to talk with Mary; the angel Michael obeyed, and Mary responded in kind by giving herself to God's Holy Spirit and a child was formed in her womb. At the appointed time Jesus was born into this world, both simple folks and kings recognized the importance of this birth.
16. Joseph was forewarned by an angel from God to flee to Egypt until he was called back to Nazareth; Joseph responded by taking his family out of harm's way.

As a man, Jesus walked those pathways that other men and women had made before his arrival. Jesus from his birth was dependent upon his family for his very life, just like you and me when we were infants in our own homes. God through Joseph and his mother Mary provided a home that protected Jesus from the weather, they put food and drink upon his table, they provided the clothes upon his back, Joseph and Mary provided the funds for them to travel to and from Jerusalem during the holy times. Joseph and Mary surrounded him with unconditional love and taught him how to read scripture. Joseph taught him a trade in which he made a living from during those years he lived in Nazareth. In a sense Jesus followed the footsteps of his Father in heaven through the footsteps of his step-father Joseph and his mother Mary for those thirty years. But Jesus was destined to blaze a whole new kind of path for mankind to follow, a path that can lead every person ever born to him and to our Father in heaven. This is the path in which you and I must now follow through life, we must leave behind our old pathways and join Jesus on this new path towards heaven, our very life and future depend on us closely following Jesus each day.

I remember on a trip out west; my friend and I were traveling through Las Vegas and we were looking for a church to attend Mass this one Sunday morning. Since, I had been to that church just a few years before, I had thought I could find this church from memory, Gladys said to stop in a gas station and ask for directions, I said no, and said I was pretty sure we were going in the right direction down the street that I had travelled several years before this trip. We never did find this church before Mass started, because I was going in the wrong direction all along. Sometimes our own pathways will take us away from Jesus at times, and other times we might cross Jesus' pathway and we might feel close to him for awhile, then our pathway again may often lead us away from Jesus and we become lost again. My pride kept me from wanting to ask for help back in Las Vegas, but when I did ask, I was put on a path that led us to the church for Mass, twenty five minutes late. Jesus says in scripture: *"I am the way and truth and life,"* [3] which means that there can be only one path to heaven and that path is through Jesus, so put your pride aside and stop and ask him for directions; for Jesus knows which way we must go in life.

Physically Jesus followed other people's pathways as he travelled from village to village, but spiritually Jesus became the new pathway for us to follow in the world, a pathway bringing us home to the Father. There is no other road to the Father except the road through Jesus. Everything in Jesus life was a reflection of the will of God, from where he travelled, to the people he called as disciples, to the people he healed, or the words he spoke, or the prayers he prayed, his suffering and death on the cross happened because it was his Father's will that he should suffer and die this way. You and I must now become a reflection of the will of God as lived through Jesus, from where we travel in life, from the people called to be a part of our lives, from the people we will heal during our lifetimes, in the words we speak each day, or in the prayer life we have with God through Jesus, and we must learn to accept God's will for those times in our life when we are called to suffer.

Jesus gave his will to his Father while being tempted in the wilderness for forty days; following this period of temptation Jesus came into Galilee and began to preach the gospel of God's love for the world. Scripture tells us right now: *"This is the time of fulfillment. The kingdom of God is at hand. Repent, and believe in the gospel."* [4] Following this proclamation of God's new kingdom, Jesus called his first disciples saying in this scripture: *"Come after me and I will make you fishers of men."* [5] Simon and Andrew responded by following Jesus immediately. The other Apostles were called in the same way by Jesus, they

---

[3]   *John 14:6a,NAB*

[4]   *Mark 1:15,NAB*

[5]   *Mark 1:17,NAB*

all turned from the direction they were going in life, leaving their old lives behind and they each began to follow Jesus along this narrow path towards a new vision of the future. When the Lord came upon a man with an unclean spirit, he says: *"Quiet! Come out of him!"*[6] The unclean spirit did as Jesus commanded and leaves this man's body. Another time, Jesus says to the paralytic man in this scripture, *"Your sins are forgiven, or to say, Rise, pick up your mat and walk?"*[7] Then the man followed the Lord's command and got up and walked in front of the other disciples and people, thus giving glory to God. In another scripture: *"Jesus calms a storm by rebuking the wind; and the sea grew calm. Jesus asks, the wind responds."*[8]

Are we seeing the picture of God's world yet? God speaks; the world responds. God speaks; Abraham and Moses responded by taking on the tasks given to them from God. God speaks; an angel responded and followed God's command. God speaks; Mary responded by allowing her body to be used as a holy vessel for the Lord's birth into the world. God speaks, and Jesus responded by teaching the world of his Father's love. Jesus speaks; an unclean spirit responded by leaving the man. Jesus speaks; a man is forgiven and the man's body responded by becoming healthy again. Jesus speaks; the wind responded to his command and quieted down. A soldier asks Jesus to heal his daughter; Jesus heals his daughter because the man demonstrated a faith that came from God, the daughter's body responded to the command and she was healed. A woman touches the hem of Jesus' robe and she was healed because of her faith in God. Jesus tells Lazarus to rise up and leave the tomb and Lazarus comes to life again and walks out of the tomb. Our lives and future in heaven depend upon our ability to hear and act upon the commands given to us by the Lord each day.

---

6   *Mark 1:25,NAB*

7   *Mark 2:9,NAB*

8   *Mark 4:39,NAB*

After the fall of Adam and Eve, because of their sin in the Garden of Eden; the world and heaven became separated from each other. It was this one act of sin that created the distance between our world and God. It wasn't God who separated Himself from us in the world because God's love for the world and us has never wavered since the dawn of time. Even today God's love remains constant for every man, woman and child despite our still sinful nature. God as our Creator has constantly told us that there is only one way to live in this world, and that is by following the will and guidance of the Lord each moment of the day. God gave us Jesus to become that bridge between the world and God, so we must accept the Lord's will over every part of our lives—in order to be purified and made ready for heaven.

When Adam and Eve ate from the tree in the Garden they truly believed that they too could become like god and be able to understand as God knew His world. Because of this one sin, the world was forever changed; this one sin has marked the soul of every child born into the world from the dawn of time. Because of their sin, God sent Adam and Eve out into the world where they now were given the opportunity for becoming their own little "god" over their environment and lives. If mankind was going to survive into the future, we needed to find a way for coming back into the presence of God, and we were given many sacred Covenants from God; which bound us to God in a special way, and we were given the Lord Jesus by God, so Jesus becomes the sign of the New Covenant of God's love.

The bible that we read today is made up of story after story of this great struggle of the people of the world trying to survive in the world of their own making. The struggle that began with Adam and Eve is still very much a part of our world today, we don't have to look far to see a world careening out of control, all because we still believe we can be as smart as God.

From the moment of creation God has loved us from the beginning of time, as He has always loved every other aspect of His creation. Because of our free will we are given a choice between following one of the now two pathways for the world: God's original pathway, or the pathway that was the result of Adam and Eve's sin. So, we must choose the path carefully, for one path takes us towards God in heaven and the other path leads us farther away from God. The narrow path of Jesus is not a free ride to heaven, but it still requires all of our strength, all of our heart, all of our mind to stay on this path going towards Jesus at the cross.

Jesus always followed the creation model: God speaks, and the world responded in kind during those seven periods or days. God spoke, Jesus responded by doing his Father's will for the world. Jesus asked those men to follow him, specific men that God wanted for His son's Apostles and disciples. Jesus taught these men the details of God's truth for the world, these men saw how much Jesus loved his Father, they saw how he prayed to his Father, they saw how God worked through Jesus in the hundreds of physical healings and as he released evil spirits and demons from those people who were possessed. Jesus gave the key to his earthly Church to Peter because he recognized that Peter proclaimed a truth that could have come only from his Father in heaven. It was the powers and sacraments from God that Jesus gave to Peter that became the foundation of his Church on earth. God chose, Jesus gave Peter the key, and Peter responded to the Lord by doing the will of Jesus in the world. God sent through Jesus the gift of the Holy Spirit, a Spirit that can now help solidify all those teachings that Jesus shared with the world, the very same Spirit that helped to empower the first Apostles and the early Church in expanding out into the world. The Church points us to Jesus, the Holy Spirit teaches us about Jesus and helps us pray to the Father, and Jesus takes us to the Father in heaven, this is the narrow path we must be on.

"If we heap titles on him, pray to him, use all the correct formulae about him, we may simply be keeping him at a distance. Yet he desires to work from within our lives. He seeks to lay claim to our hearts, to eternally disturb

us, to whisper to us about perfection. He asks us to believe that he is still passionately involved in our lives, that he is still healing us, making us whole by troubling us and challenging us to be different." [9]

At the age of thirty two, I was testing a call to the priesthood; I attended a seminary where I began taking courses towards a Master's degree. On the seminary property was a prayer pathway that the seminarians in the past had used for praying, but the pathway had been allowed to become overgrown with fallen branches and heavy brush, so this Bishop's prayer path had become useless to the seminarians for a number of years. I got permission from the rector to begin clearing away the brush and limbs from this pathway during my free time and after several weeks the pathway was now useable again. I was told that some of the seminarians made fun of me for working so hard on this pathway. I didn't mind their musings because I didn't complete this task for my own glorification, I did it to honor God and Jesus, because we are all called to love and serve others and we are asked to live out our lives in a certain way which can give glory to God. I also cleaned this pathway as a way to honor all those men who had gone before me in studying for the priesthood, and to honor all those families who had supported the seminary for years with their generous gifts of money and time. Following Christ is hard work at times, we don't often know where Jesus will take us in life, or the people we will meet along the way, but I know that some men were touched by my efforts on clearing this prayer pathway, perhaps they were brought closer to Jesus in some way, certainly as they used this pathway again during their prayer time with the Lord.

Jesus preached constantly about God's new Gospel, to his disciples, to the people wherever he walked during his ministry

---

[9]   *P.14, excerpt used from "Disturbing the Peace," Eamonn Bredin, Columbia Press, The Rise, Mount Merrion, Blackrock, Co., Dublin, Ireland, 1991, used with permission, (www.cup.columbia.edu)*

years, to the people he dined with each day, Jesus taught in the Temple, he taught on a hillside, he taught from a boat, he taught through his prayers to God, he taught by his daily actions, he taught by his giving his body and blood to his disciples at the Last Supper, he taught by being courageous during his arrest, trial and suffering, he taught about God before his death on the cross, he taught by dying on the cross, he taught through his risen body after Easter morning, and even today the Lord continues to teach us each day through his many acts of grace and truth.

The first Apostles, aside from his mother Mary knew Jesus better than anyone else in the world, through these special men called by God through Jesus; they became the repository of all his teachings and actions. Scripture tells us quite clearly that these same Apostles didn't always fully understand all these teachings that Jesus shared and demonstrated with them during those two or three life changing years that they walked with Jesus. It wasn't until after Jesus' death on the cross and his return to heaven, whereby God through Jesus gave the world the Holy Spirit, only then did the Apostle's eyes and hearts become open up to the many teachings of God's Gospel.

The people of Israel were clearly expecting a Savior for their world, but many of these folks had different ideas on what that Savior would look like. Eleven of the Apostles and half of the Lord's disciples accepted and recognized Jesus as their Savior and Messiah. Judas Iscariot had a different vision for Jesus as the Savior of Israel, so he was willing to betray Jesus and have him arrested. Scripture tells us that about half of the Lord's disciples left Jesus at one point because they too had a different vision of Jesus; they couldn't believe the words that Jesus spoke on certain truths of their faith. Both God and Jesus always knew which disciples would leave the path that Jesus calls us to live on each day, these disciples left because they could not accept the idea of being asked to eat the body and blood of the Lord.

This group of the Lord's disciples was not the only folks who had a hard time accepting the many truths that Jesus was sharing with the people of Israel. The Pharisees also had a different vision of what a Messiah should look like in their world, as did the Zealots, as did the Sadducees, and even the Romans viewed Jesus in a different manner than what the religious folks believed.

In the movie "Forrest Gump," there was this part where Forrest begins to run across the country as a way to think through his disappointment with a lost love, eventually Forrest had a big following of people who ran with him across the country; all believing that Forrest had some deep insights into life and how the world all fits together. Along this one long sloping stretch in the mountains with maybe a hundred people following him, Forrest stops, everybody else stops and waits for some deep revelation from Forrest, which they hope will give them deep meaning and purpose to their lives. Forrest turns around on the road and faces home, and says to the people that he was tired and that he wanted to go home, and so he begins walking towards home. The people are dumb founded and disappointed because they saw in Forrest something different, it would seem that a man with enough commitment for running over eight thousand miles across the country would be a person worthy to follow and learn from in life. They too had a different view of a man who they thought had all the answers about life.[10]

"The Jews quarreled among themselves, saying, 'How can this man give us (his) flesh to eat?' Jesus said to them, 'Amen, amen, I say to you, unless you eat the flesh of the Son of Man and drink his blood, you do not have life within you. Whoever eats my flesh and drinks my blood has eternal life, and I will raise him on the last day, for my flesh is true food, and my blood is true drink. Whoever eats my flesh and drinks my blood

---

[10]   *Forrest Gump, written by Winston Groom, Director, Robert Zemeckis, Paramount Pictures, 1994 (paraphrased description of small section in movie, no actual quotes used)*

remains in me and I in him. Just as the living Father sent me and I have life because of the Father, so also the one who feeds on me will have life because of me. This is the bread that came down from heaven. Unlike your ancestors who ate and still died, whoever eats this bread will live forever.' These things he said while teaching in the synagogue in Capernaum."

"Then many of his disciples who were listening said, 'This saying is hard; who can accept it?' Since Jesus knew that his disciples were murmuring about this, he said to them, 'Does this shock you? What if you were to see the Son of Man ascending to where he was before? It is the spirit that gives life, while the flesh is of no avail. The words I have spoken to you are spirit and life. But there are some of you who do not believe. Jesus knew from the beginning the ones who would not believe and the one who would betray him.'"

"And he said, 'For this reason I have told you that no one can come to me unless it is granted him by my Father.' As a result of this, many (of) his disciples returned to their former way of life and no longer accompanied him. Jesus then said to the Twelve, 'Do you also want to leave?' Simon Peter answered him, 'Master, to whom shall we go? You have the words of eternal life. We have come to believe and are convinced that you are the Holy One of God.' Jesus answered them, 'Did I not choose you twelve? Yet is not one of you a devil?' He was referring to Judas, son of Simon the Iscariot; it was he who would betray him, one of the Twelve." [11]

I have always wondered what happened to those disciples who left Jesus that day, what happened with their lives, did

---

[11]   *John 6:52-71, NAB*

they ever find their way back to Jesus? What kept them from being known by God? God chooses who comes to Jesus, from His mother, to the Apostles, to His disciples, to those who were healed by God through Jesus.

God didn't send Jesus out to preach to a specific area of society, he preached to people of all kinds, from the super rich and down to the poorest of the poor. His message was given to both men and women who followed all of God's laws and to those men and women who were lost in the hardness of life, including their own sins. So why does God's message touch some lives, while others aren't affected by the Lord's message? I think the parable of the seeds falling on good soil and rocky soils answers this question for us. The disciples who left Jesus that day, left because they were not ready to respond to this new life in Christ. God knew that these disciples were not ready to receive Jesus fully into their lives, so these disciples returned to their old pathways with all its comforts and surety of direction, a pathway that didn't challenge them to grow in their faith and knowledge of God.

The pathway to heaven is through but one single man, born of a woman, son of God, given to the world for a single purpose. Both you and I must now answer the Lord's question right now? "Do you also want to leave?" Can you accept all my teachings as God wants? Jesus tells us in this scripture: *"Amen, amen, I say to you, unless you eat the flesh of the Son of Man and drink his blood, you do not have life within you. Whoever eats my flesh and drinks my blood has eternal life, and I will raise him on the last day."[12]* I think there was much confusion among the Apostles as they came to grasp all the many facets of God's plan for the world, for we can read scripture after scripture that points out this type of confusion for the Lord's disciples.

Let us think about our last visit to the doctor, we went through a series of medical tests, the doctor examined the results and prescribed a certain plan for us that addresses our

---

[12]   *John 6:53-54, NAB*

health issue, whether it is surgery, medicine or a combination of both. The doctor will often use words that are highly technical and unfamiliar to us, words that we don't fully understand. More than likely we would tell the doctor to go ahead with their medical plan, even though we don't fully understand all the details. We know we have a medical problem that needs to be addressed, so we place our trust and faith in the doctor because of their medical training and skills they have developed over the years. It isn't until later that we begin to understand our medical condition more fully, because we had just devoted some extra time towards researching our disease and the steps we need to take to correct our health issue.

Do you remember in scripture when Peter was walking towards Jesus on the water? As long as he kept his eyes on Jesus he did fine, but when he turned his eyes away from Jesus he began to sink. God is our doctor, He knows our every thought and action in life, both good and bad, and God has given us a plan for us to follow in correcting our sinful nature. It is our sinful nature that is getting in the way of our true purpose for the world, so we must first be cured of this great illness that is destroying our soul. Sometimes the truth of His words are hard for us to bear because they cut deep down into our soul, and sometimes the medicine we must take is often very bitter for us to taste, but we must stick with the plan that our Doctor has for our life.

Our only pathway to God is in following Jesus through our every breath, word and action. Jesus reminds us in this scripture about making the right choice: *"Enter through the narrow gate, for the gate is wide and the road is broad that leads to destruction, and those who enter through it are many. How narrow the gate and constricted the road that leads to life. And those who find it are few."*[13]

Can you and I find this gate and travel down this narrow path to a new life? Jesus died on the cross to give us the opportunity

---

[13]   *Matt.7:13-14,NAB*

to bridge our world with heaven, and we have to go through Jesus to get to that new life. We have to learn to look through the Lord's eyes, and not use our own eyes, and Jesus has to speak through us into the world, so we must not use our own voices. As we give our lives to Jesus, Jesus will now use our hands and feet in serving the people of our little corner of the world. We become that light which points others towards Jesus, through Jesus we become the teacher, the healer, the forgiver of sins. This new life is filled with so many blessings if we but just listen to and respond to Jesus within our soul. Jesus says we can come to think of God as our Father, and himself as our brother, which means we are a family, with bonds of love so tight that we should never feel alone again in life.

Many years ago I taught high school seniors in a Catechism class at my local parish, I spent a great deal of time teaching the students about Jesus, covering topics like prayer, the Sacraments, Holy Scripture, about the Trinity, and about how we can build up our relationship with Jesus. I used a trust exercise, where the students would be given a chance to walk across a busy highway while being blind folded and guided by a friend. As Christians we are called to place our trust in Jesus as he guides us down the narrow path, knowing that only Jesus will get us through those hard moments in life.

The Catholic Church founded by Jesus has declared that certain men and women throughout history have indeed followed Jesus down the path and entered the narrow gate. We call them Saints because they have demonstrated by their lives that they lived their life through Jesus Christ:

1. Their lives were given over to Jesus
   a. Some Saints had lived their whole lives with a pure heart
   b. While some other Saints had turned their lives away from sin and began a whole new life following Jesus
2. They lived lives of holiness
3. They lived lives of deep prayer

4. They lived lives of service to others
5. They lived lives of teaching their world about Jesus
6. They lived lives of healing other people's lives
7. Their every action and moment in life was given over to Jesus

Each person in the world will have that moment in their life where they are brought face-to-face with Jesus, a moment where we will be asked to choose which pathway they will follow through life:

1. Will it be the narrow path of Jesus Christ?
2. Or will it be the wide road of the world?

3. Will you accept God's love and grace?
4. Or will you choose to live apart from God?

Remember that trust exercise I used with my catechism class, I was the first person going across that busy road, blind folded and scared to death. I trusted the senior student completely, but since I have a very poor balance because of my neurological disease, plus stepping up or down from the curb was especially scary for me even with my eyes open. In doing this trust exercise I feared both for myself and the other person, but we made it across safely. There are many reasons why people find it hard to place their lives into another person's hands, but the world has also given us thousands of different excuses as to why we choose not to follow the Lord's path.

Saints like Padre Pio and the Cure' of Ars had both chosen to follow Jesus along this path, their every thought and word came from Jesus; their every action was given to them from Jesus. Jesus gave both men a gift for healing people's hearts for they both spent up to twenty hours a day in the confessional, seven days a week. Jesus allowed both men to struggle through the night in fighting off demons who were trying to distract both men from the work of Jesus. Jesus became such a part of their lives, their every breath and action had become the breath and action of Jesus as they lived and served the people that God had brought to them in their parish. We each have our own specific place in the world, a place where God chose us to live and work. Whether we choose to follow Jesus down that narrow path becomes dependent upon our own willingness to place our trust in God's will for us each day. Why do so many people choose to take the wide road away from Jesus during their lifetimes and not join Jesus on this pathway to God? Jesus says in this scripture: *"For this reason I have told you that no one can come to me unless it is granted him by my Father."*[14] Is this the reason why so few people follow Jesus along this narrow path? Is it because our Father hasn't given us permission to follow Jesus? Or is it because our Father knows us so intimately, that He recognizes our many strengths and gifts that He has given to us and also God is very much aware of all those sinful areas that still control our life. He knows that we are not quite ready to follow His son Jesus along this narrow path, for we have not yet come to be in that place in our life where we recognize that we are no longer at the center of the universe, but that God is our center.

As a young man my mind wasn't always on God, much of my effort was in trying to figure out what I should do with the rest of my life, working part-time, taking classes, etc. Sure, I still attended church each Sunday, but my faith was not the focus of my life. It wasn't until I was barely holding on to my life during my early twenties that God knew my heart was ready for Jesus. So, Jesus came into my life in a big way after I gave him my life and future, his love and grace began to transform every part of my life. God placed me on that narrow pathway towards the cross, it is a pathway that I now have to choose every day and re-choose every moment of each day as I follow Jesus.

Is the pathway that Christ has made for us easy to follow? How could it be, just look at what Jesus lived through on the way

---

[14]   *John 6:65, NAB*

to the cross, his pathway was filled with pain and it required every ounce of strength that he could muster as he carried his cross to Golgotha. There will be times in your life where you will feel that closeness with the Lord, and there will be times when you feel you have been abandoned by the Lord, but this is a natural stage of our faith in God. Even Jesus felt abandoned by his Father at one point; Jesus said this in his final struggle as he was hanging on the cross: *"My God, My God, why have you forsaken me?"*[15] Jesus didn't change his pathway because he felt abandoned by God, but he accepted his Father's will for his life and died willingly on the cross..

Remember the parable of the seeds falling on rocks, either the hard ground or the good soil? So it is easy to see how this parable is so easily understood by people, we know that a seed landing on good soil has a better chance for growing into a new plant, than a seed that landed on top of a rock. We recognize that each seed has the potential for producing new life as it grows in the soil, in time this seed will grow into a plant and thus be able to bear fruit—which may become food for the person's table, or the fruit of this plant can be saved for next year's planting of crops. Have you ever travelled through a mountainous area and noticed those trees growing up from what looks like rocks on the side of the mountain, one lonely tree reaching upward towards the heavens? From the roadside we can't really see where the tree is truly growing from, but if we could crawl up beside this tree we would see that there is dirt within the rock cracks from which the tree sprouted from on this mountain side, dirt that has been collecting there for thousands of years from the dust blowing against the mountain. The miracle of dirt is that it provides food and nutrients to the seeds that are planted within it; and the success for any new plant is whether there is enough rain falling from the heavens and light from the Sun to activate the growing process.

---

[15]   *Matt.27:46b,NAB*

Whether we follow the narrow path of Christ or we follow another path away from God, or whether our seed falls on good soil, or our seed falls on a rocky ground, what needs to take place from our point of view is what we must now decide what to do with our free will. If we give to Jesus our free will, we are placing our complete trust and faith in him, giving him our past, present and future. If we choose to keep our free will and travel down a different road, we must also accept the consequences for that decision, a road that is ultimately devoid of God. If we are on this wide road moving away from God we must also know that there will be many opportunities for us to exit this road and begin a new life with Christ. Unlike the toll roads around the country exiting off the wide road of the world doesn't cost you money, Jesus offers us a free token, and he paid for it with his death on the cross.

"However if we are really convinced that this is God's work, that it is about the future impinging on our present, then it necessarily involves both the radically new and the not-yet. Discipleship must always involve us in a profound but usually unacknowledged, not knowing. It means that we who choose and daily re-choose the path of discipleship must always move beyond what has been achieved, to acknowledge that there is much we do not know" [16]

---

[16]   *P.11, excerpt used from "Disturbing the Peace," Eamonn Bredin, Columbia Press, The Rise, Mount Merrion, Blackrock, Co., Dublin, Ireland, 1991, used with permission, (www.cup.columbia.edu)*

CHAPTER 2

THE FREEWAY

In our last chapter we explored the importance of the narrow pathway as it related to our lives with Jesus, in this chapter we need to understand what the wide road, or the freeway means for our world. The scripture suggests that most people choose to take this wide road as they live in God's world, and very few people find their way through this small gate and onto this narrow pathway. In the last chapter, we explored how hard it was to follow this narrow path towards Christ, and how it took all of our commitment and effort to stay on this path. So we need to discover why it is that so many people choose the wide road of the world and maybe we can begin to recognize the many dangers along this wide road, so we can keep our eyes more clearly towards Christ on the path.

God doesn't say there are many roads to heaven, there is only one path to God, and that it is through our Lord Jesus Christ. I remember as a child my parents took us kids on a trip to California to see our great-aunts Blanche and Edith out in Los Angeles. The majority of our trip west we primarily drove down the Interstate highways for they were much faster than traveling the State routes. Most Interstate highways are usually made up of four lanes, with two lanes going in one direction, while the other two lanes went in the opposite direction. When we wanted to see certain scenic sites, or find a motel or a place to eat, my dad would now drive his car off the Interstate and onto a normal two lane road, either a State route or a County road. These State routes are usually made up of two lanes that travel in the opposite directions of each other, whether north or south, or east and west. I remember one time my dad pulled the car off one of these two lane highways and went on a road my younger sister called a "punched out" road, really nothing more than a dirt or gravel road, something we might have called back home, a country lane. Basically it was a road used by very few people, "off the beaten path" as my dad called it. As we travelled into the Los Angeles area we came in on my first major freeway, it was a highway made up of eight lanes, with four lanes of highway going in both directions, and the freeway was capable of moving hundreds of thousands of cars along its pavement over the course of the day. We learned pretty quickly when to use the freeway and when to stay off the freeway, especially during rush hour.

So far we have talked about an eight lane Freeway, a four lane Interstate highway, a two lane State route, a two lane County roads, (either blacktop or gravel). We also have other roads we can travel on: like a one and one-half lane Township roads; which are narrower and usually are made up of gravel. Another type of a road is a one lane farm lane, where generally the only people who travel down this lane are the people who live at the end of this lane, my first home was at the end of such a long lane. I used to walk on a walking path in going through various local parks, the path was mostly made up of dirt, but in some cases the path was made out of black top. In the area behind my parent's house in Tiskilwa, there was a hillside where cattle grazed in a field below our house; the cattle would follow a cow path up and down the hillside as they moved to different feeding areas of this timber area. I have several friends who can track a deer through the woods just by following their hoof marks and my brothers could track rabbits in the woods by following their tiny feet.

I think that we who live today have a hard time understanding the words of scripture as they relate to the narrow pathway or the wide road talked about in scripture. I think we recognize the wide "freeway" today is capable of handling thousands and thousands of people at a time, whereas the narrow pathway can probably only handle just one or two people at a time. We know this wide freeway is made up of either concrete or blacktop material, while this narrow path was most likely made of a combination of dirt, rocks, leaves and roots, with trees and plants nearby or flanking the pathway. We understand that one path is hard and one road is easy to navigate, but, we must learn to understand the terms for these words in the context of the time that Jesus lived and breathed.

Jesus primarily travelled by foot everywhere he walked as a young child or as a young man while he worked for his step-father Joseph, but especially when Jesus began his ministry at the age of thirty. The roads he travelled were really more like pathways, rough, made of rock, or most likely dirt paths that were made hard by years of people and animals trampling the path down. Surely on occasion Jesus could have travelled the major caravan routes, and even some of the roads the Romans made through that area of Israel. But we must realize that it took much effort for a person to travel by foot anywhere in Israel. There was the effort in walking up and down mountain paths, the effort in walking over rough and dangerous terrain. It is estimated that a person can walk twenty miles a day, most Americans today would find it hard to walk these twenty miles, especially if the temperatures were high in the desert heat, and especially when travelling on these pathways through the mountains.

So, why do most people choose the easiest path, or as scripture says in Matthew 7, that most people travel on the wide road leading to our own destruction? Is it our weak human nature that puts us on these wide roads? Is it because as humans we always seek the fastest ways of reaching a goal? In the high school I attended as a young man, if we wanted to eat our school lunch, we had to walk over from the high school and travel several blocks on our way to the grade school cafeteria. We were told to follow the sidewalks to and from the high school, but most of the kids would cut through people's yards on our way to and from the grade school, for we chose this way because it was shorter and faster.

How many of us would choose the stairway for going up thirty floors in a building, instead of using an elevator? On a personal level if we had a choice, which person would you rather experience? 1) A mother dying of cancer, surrounded by people they loved 2) or a woman dying alone is some hospital bed far from her only daughter and a husband who had abandoned her a few years before. I can guess that most people would choose to be that woman dying surrounded by the people they loved. I can go through hundreds of these kinds of examples that demonstrate why we as humans usually choose the easier and wider path.

Let us explore Matthew 7:13-14 in greater detail to help us understand why so many choose the wide road, leading to our destruction: *"Enter through the narrow gate; for the gate is wide and the road broad that leads to destruction; and those who enter through it are many. How narrow the gate and constricted the road that leads to life. And those who find it are few."[17]*

Most parents would give their child what they ask for within reason, my wife Rowena as a child asked her mother for an onion when she was sick, and she got it. When we wore out our shoes as a child, our parents would buy us another pair to wear. When my sister Sandy had a bicycle accident and she broke her leg, my parents brought her to the emergency room. As a child, if we asked my mother for a candy in the checkout lane in a grocery store, she would have probably said no to our request, nor would she have offered us cigarettes or alcohol as a child either.

The scripture suggests we should look beyond our most basic of needs as to what a good parent or what an evil parent would provide for us as children. The good gifts given to us by our heavenly Father are far different than the ones our parents can give us. God is telling us that we need to ask Him for those good gifts that can truly better each of our lives. We also know that it is only through Jesus can we come to know the Father and ask for these good gifts. As a child nobody knows us better

---

[17]   *Matt.7:13-14,NAB*

than our parents do, so we can be sure our heavenly Father knows us even better than our parents ever could. As a child I loved my parents fully, it doesn't mean I knew them fully as individuals, but I did trust in their love for me. Can we know our Father in heaven in the same way we knew our own parents? We can learn about our Father only through what Jesus can give us:

1. Following the narrow pathway towards Jesus at the cross at Calvary
2. Through the understanding of the Lord's teachings on God
3. Through the reading of the Holy Scripture
4. Through the guidance of the Holy Spirit
5. Through the teaching of the Catholic Church that Jesus formed through Peter.
6. Through the sacraments of grace given us from Jesus through the Church
7. Through our daily prayer with the Lord

As an infant we cried when we needed food, or cried when we needed to have our diaper changed, this cry was our way to communicate to our parents our needs. In the same way we need to learn how to communicate with our heavenly Father and ask Him what we need for our lives. Jesus calls this prayer. I have worked with hundreds of children over the years, some of them who couldn't say a word, but every child demonstrated an ability to express their love to you, and each child had the ability for letting us know about their physical needs. My little cat Tabitha loves to curl up on my shoulder, she purrs and demonstrates to me her love.

How can we ever come to know our Father in heaven when we don't talk with Him and tell Him of our love for Him? Our Father in heaven knows what we need before we ask, but I am afraid most of us don't take the time to truly seek out our Father each day and ask Him about our needs for the day, nor do we take the time and show God our thankfulness and love for all that He has given to us within our lives.

The Lord gives us an important truth in this scripture: *"Do to others whatever you would have them do to you. This is the law and the prophets."*[18] So, if you want to be loved by others, then love others purely. If you wanted kindness shown you, than be kind to everyone you meet. If you want to be hated by others, then show hatred towards those people in your life. If you want mercy, then be merciful to others in your life.

As a teacher in a high school I often heard others students calling their friends retarded as they walked down the hallways, just past our door. When I could and certainly not every time I would ask the students to watch what they are saying to each other. Most of the students within my wing knew that the word retarded has a negative and degrading meaning as its being used. Even some of my own students recognized the hurtful nature of these words when spoken by others, and on several occasions I have heard a couple of my own student's use this term in calling another classmate retarded. I would pull them aside and discuss with them the hurtful nature of this word and why we shouldn't use these types of words in that way. I tried to help them learn other ways to express their feelings or anger towards those people they didn't like. I provided opportunities for my students to practice in being civil with one another, and in showing respect to one another; it was a lesson that many of the "normal" students had yet to understand.

Our world is filled with many examples of great acts of love and mercy, from the world's responses to any natural disaster like hurricanes, tornadoes, flooding or fires, feeding the poor around the world, providing medical care to the poor around the world. But then, we have all those other stories in our newspapers that bring the most harm into the world, impacting lives at the deepest of levels:

---

[18]   *Matt.7:12,NAB*

1. Countries at war
2. People killing each other with guns or other acts of violence
3. People who are victims of rape
4. People who steal from others
5. People struggling with the hopelessness of poverty
6. All those people lost in their own world through their own self-destructive pursuits
   a. drug abuse
   b. alcoholism
   c. sexual perversions
   d. a lust for power and/or money

Every day at school I saw a growing lack of respect for others, towards their peers, towards staff and towards the school. If you drive down any road in the country you can see the roadsides are littered with trash that people have thrown out their car windows. And you see this lack of respect by the way so many pets are being abused and abandoned by their owners. We have people who are also being abandoned by their families and friends, living alone in nursing homes, alone in their homes, or along the streets of our cities. Our world is filled with refugees and orphans in the many countries at war. Is there any hope for us in this world? No wonder many people just want to crawl back in bed and pull the covers over their heads. Our heavenly Father has told us that our hope only lies with His son Jesus Christ, so follow him, and accept his love and mercy, and accept his will for you in this world.

"My son, if you receive my words and treasure my commands, Turning your ear to wisdom, inclining your heart to understanding; Yes, if you call to intelligence, and to understanding raise your voice; If you seek her like silver, and like hidden treasures search her out: Then will you understand the fear of the Lord; the knowledge of God you will find; For the Lord gives wisdom, from his mouth come knowledge and

understanding; He has counsel in store for the upright, he is the shield of those who walk honestly, Guarding the paths of justice, protecting the way of his pious ones. Then you will understand rectitude and justice, honesty, every good path; For wisdom will enter your heart, knowledge will please your soul, Discretion will watch over you, understanding will guard you; Saving you from the way of evil men, from men of perverse speech, Who leave the straight paths to walk in the way of darkness, Who delight in doing evil, rejoice in perversity; Whose ways are crooked, and devious their paths;" [19]

Narrow Path vs. the Broad Road

Again we are being reminded in this scripture of the need to make a choice: *"Enter through the narrow gate; for the gate is wide and the road broad that leads to destruction and those who enter through it are many."* [20] Growing up on a farm we had two types of gates, a narrow gate and a wider gate, the narrow gate allowed one animal to pass through at a time into another pen, we used this narrow gate to sort out the pigs going to market, only a certain size of a hog went through the narrow gate, those pigs that made it through the gate were allowed to stay with us a little longer on the farm, in order to be fattened up some more before they were sent off to market. The wider gate was used to allow more animals to come in and out of other lots, or from the fields, coming in together at the same time. This wide gate also allowed our tractor to come in and out of the feeding lot. These gates had to be opened by another person, so the tractor and wagon could pass out of the lot without any cattle or pigs escaping.

---

[19]   *Prov.2:1-15,NAB*

[20]   *Matt.7:13,NAB*

In Jerusalem, the city was a walled fortress that had both kinds of gates as well. The larger gates were generally kept open during the day, except during the time of war, for this gate allowed a greater number of people to pass in and out of the city at the same time, including their animals and the goods strapped upon the animal's back, goods the people were bringing in to sell at the street market. The smaller gates didn't allow larger animals to pass through, only people. The funny things about gates is that we need to make a choice in whether to open the gate or not, and if it is opened, we must make a conscious decision to walk through the gate and enter the city. The hallways at the school I worked at could handle about four people wide at a time walking side-by-side, maybe five wide, and each day at lunch time we would experience a large number of students either going to the cafeteria or leaving the cafeteria for their classes, anyway it is about two hundred students converging on the cafeteria and two hundred students leaving the cafeteria. An interesting phenomenon occurs during the hot season when the double doors are closed in order for the central area of the school to be air conditioned. If our class opened up the right side door, those kids coming from the other side of the door might try and squeeze through this opened door as we are walking through, or the students would stop and pile up in numbers as they waited for our class to finish going through the door we had just opened, and when our class passed by the students would now head towards this opened door and on they would go towards the cafeteria. These students didn't have to squeeze through our door as we went through, nor did they have to wait until our class made it through this door, they could have opened up the door on their side of the hallway, but no, they always waited for the moment that they could go through the open door. Is the reason why so many people go through the wide gate and travel down the wide road is because the door is open and more people are going in that direction? Because so many other people are following what others are doing and not thinking for themselves.

My brother John lives near Tucson, it is flanked by a mountain called Mt. Lemon, it is a beautiful and cool place to retreat to during the hot season, it has a two lane highway going all the way up the mountain, and it is a nice and scenic ride going up to the top. But there is another way up to the top of the mountain and that is a rough gravel and dirt road, and at times the path or road is filled with huge boulders that needed to be traversed over on our way up or down the mountain. You could walk up this rough road, or you can drive an all terrain vehicle up to the top, it was one long and arduous trip filled with many dangers, but the excitement was heightened and the views were beautiful as well. But 99.9% of the people who go up Mt. Lemon will always choose to take the easy road up this mountain, instead of the narrow pathway up the mountain.

The scripture says we must choose to enter the narrow gate, taking you on a narrow path that is far different than the wide gate and road that will lead to our eventual destruction.

1. Small gate, which is a narrow road that leads to life; and only a few will find it—heaven
2. Wide gate, which is a broad road that leads to our destruction; and many, will enter this gate—hell

I think the key words in these scriptures from Matthew are "only a few find it." I grew up in a home where we went to church every Sunday, and we attended catechism on Saturdays to learn about our faith and our Catholic Church. We partook of the sacraments of the Catholic Church. I had all these graces from the Lord, but I still did not understand fully their impact upon my life. I guess what I am trying to say, is that with all these graces and knowledge that I gained from catechism and Mass each Sunday I still couldn't find the small gate to enter and begin my journey on this narrow path. It took God's plan for me to grow weak from my disease for me to open my eyes and find this gate. For the first time in my life I began in earnest to seek out answers within my world, through books, through the Catholic Church and through prayer, and my journey truly began along this narrow path to God.

Your Fruit You Will Recognize Them:

Definition for True Prophet: "In religion, a prophet is an individual who is claimed to have been contacted by the supernatural or the divine, and to speak for them, serving as an intermediary with humanity, delivering this newfound knowledge from the supernatural entity to other people." [21]

Definition for False Prophet: "But if a prophet presumes to speak in my name an oracle that I have not commanded him to speak, or speaks in the name of other gods, he shall die." [22]

A true prophet speaks about God because God commanded it of him or her. We have many prophets who speak about the will of God for our lives, but they were not commanded by God to speak on His behalf. There is a distinct difference between these two types of prophets, the first one Jesus says is a prophet in sheep's clothing, their motive isn't to lift you up and protect you, but to draw you in and turn you from the true path of God, while the true prophet is doing the will of the heavenly Father. How can we tell the two kinds of prophets apart from each other? Jesus says we can recognize them by the kind of fruits they bring into the world. How can we learn to tell the difference between what is a good fruit and what is a bad fruit for our lives? It is much more than testing to see if the fruit is rotten and then throwing it away, or whether the fruit is perfect and fit to eat. I think if we are following Christ on

---

[21] *Data taken from (http://en.wikipedia.org/wiki/Prophet)*

[22] *Deut.18:20,NAB*

the narrow pathway we can easily see what is good or bad for us, not because of our own judgment, but because we can trust in knowing what God wants for us in our lives. And if we are walking on the wide path, our ability for deciding what is good or bad for us is dependent on our own idea or what we think that God wants, but it may also be in accord with what other people are doing on the wider road.

We are not alone in this world for we have God as our Father, we have Jesus as our brother, we have the Holy Spirit who is our teacher, and we have the Catholic Church that Jesus formed through the Apostle Peter and the other eleven Apostles. It was the early Catholic Church who wrote and formed the scriptures that we call today the New Testament. It was through their devotion and the working of the Holy Spirit who helped form the words for these scriptures, words that were first given to them from Jesus. It was the early Catholic Church who continued to preach the words that Jesus gave them during those three years of Jesus' ministry. Christ commanded them to go out two-by-two into the countryside and preach the Good News of God, to heal and serve the people, showing them the way to God. Jesus gave us seven sacraments in which the Church gives to its people as a sign of God's continued grace and mercy.

But God doesn't stop there either, God gave us Mary, who is the mother of Jesus, the same Jesus we can call our brother, which also means Mary is our mother as well. God has given us many people we can look up to and learn from, people like Saint Padre Pio, Saint Francis, Billy Graham, or Pope John Paul II, and so many others. We have angels that guide and protect us throughout our lifetimes, and God gives us certain people within our lives who will touch our hearts in a deep spiritual way; people like our parents and family members, or our spouse, or our best friends, or our local parish priest or ministers, or our children.

The Key:

Father Lauer once said at Mass, that if every Christian actually lived as Christ intended for us to live, then our world would have no war, no crimes, no poverty, and our world now would be one of peace.[23] So, he asked us to allow the Holy Spirit to look deep within our heart and bring to our attention to those areas of our life that have kept us from knowing Jesus more fully in our lives. Fr. Lauer is saying that our failure to make an impact in this world as a follower of Christ; is because we haven't yet given Jesus every aspect of our lives, even those areas of our lives that we have hidden away from others. But, Jesus knows what those areas are in our life anyway, for nothing is hidden from the Jesus. But the Lord won't take them out of our life until we are ready to give these sins and hidden areas to him at the cross. If we are living on the wide road of the world, it is because of our desire to remain in control over our lives as best we can each day.

---

[23] *Father Lauer was a Catholic Priest from Cincinnati, OH, he was one of the founding members of Presentation Ministries, his words and thoughts were from a homily he spoke at a Mass I attended in Springfield, IL.(paraphrased)*

CHAPTER 3

THE WORLD AND OUR PLACE IN IT!

"This is how you are to pray: Our Father in heaven, hallowed be your name, your kingdom come, your will be done, on earth as in heaven. Give us today our daily bread; and forgive us our debts, as we forgive our debtors; and do not subject us to the final test, but deliver us from the evil one." [24]

Jesus gives to each of us our daily bread, whether we choose to receive this food becomes our choice to make each day. When we accept this bread into our lives, our faith is nourished and strengthened by this gift, and when we refuse or ignore this bread, our faith becomes weakened.

My wife Rowena's favorite vegetable has always been the onion, she eats it at most every meal. As a child when she was sick, she would ask her mother to get her an onion and she would eat it like an apple and then she would feel comforted. The onion is a good tool in which we can learn more about our faith and how we can grow closer to God. Have you ever cut an onion in half and noticed how the onion has many layers that circle the center part of the onion where the immature flower would sprout from when planted in your garden?

Every person ever born comes into the world living under specific circumstances and different family situations which help shape how we grow and interact with the world; it is these circumstances and situations that form within us layer upon layer of various beliefs and attitudes, like an onion, and often these learned beliefs and attitudes will then affect the way we

---

[24]   *Matt.6:9-13,NAB*

interact with our world. I met someone once who grew up in a home where their parents taught their kids from an early age how to fight and steal from others. Another family, their parents taught their kids about the love one has for the family, about the love for their friends, about the love they have their neighbors, about the love they have for their country and about the love they have for one's own faith in God. Did both families demonstrate love and care for their kids? Did both families provide shelter, food and warmth for their children? I am sure both families provided these things in their own unique way according to their own sets of circumstances.

"Amen, amen, I say to you, unless a grain of wheat falls to the ground and dies, it remains just a grain of wheat; but if it dies, it produces much fruit. Whoever loves his life loses it; and whoever hates his life in this world will preserve it for eternal life. Whoever serves me must follow me, and where I am, there also will my servant be. The Father will honor whoever serves me." [25]

When we look at the onion again we can see layer after layer of skin that protects the inner core of the onion where the flower originates, which is the source for the new life of the onion. It is common to keep an onion in a cool dark place, so they will stay fresh longer. Even in a dark room and over time these same onions will grow mushy and a sprout will push up through the bulb towards any source of light. When left alone the onion will continue to soften, and the flower will dry up and you would end up with just a ruined onion. But when that same onion is taken and planted in to some soil, new life will grow from this seed, and in time this plant will produce some new fruit.

When we don't use our faith, allowing it to waste away like a rotten onion, we become useless to God, but when we allow

---

[25]   *John12:24-26,NAB*

God to plant us in a new ground, we are given a chance for a new life. It is through God's action within our life that we are given opportunities to live a new life through His son Jesus Christ. In order for this to happen we must give to Jesus our very life, giving him those many, many layers of the onion that surrounds and protects our core, a core that has been infused with a soul that was given to us by God at our conception. If you carved the flower out of the onion after it sprouted in your pantry, and placed it into the ground, it would probably dry out quickly and never sprout. This seed died because it still lacked something very important to its survival—it lacked the many layers that surrounded the core of the seed which is the center of the onion, it is these layers that must die and provide the nourishment for the seed to be reborn into a flower, into a whole new life capable of bearing good fruit for the world.

Every person ever born has a special message for the world, a message learned from our interactions with the people in our world and from what we have learned from life and our Lord Jesus. I once held an 18 year old man the size of an infant during a volunteer experience for a class I was taking in college, Steven wasn't able to tell you his message in words, but you could be a witness to his message by how he lived out his life each day, in complete trust in God's love for him as a man. This man's message for the world is as important as mine or any other person ever born. Jesus died for Steven, and he has died for every other person born into this world, dying for our loved ones, dying for our enemies, and he even died for you and me.

When that message from each person is united to Christ the message now has an opportunity to teach other people about God's love for the world, and when the message stands apart from Jesus that message will then dry out and die quickly. This doesn't mean that we should dismiss those people of other faiths for it was God who placed these people in that part of the world. No longer can we say we are better than others, for we are all loved by our Father in heaven, we all have equal value, so we all must be guided by Jesus and be willing to respect all people as our siblings in Christ. The Pharisees had difficulty with Jesus because he associated with "the sinners" of the world, Jesus treated every person with love and respect, for it didn't matter if they were saints or sinners, for Jesus loved each individual unconditionally, as a brother or a sister, as a person who was very important to God. We should do no less than live in the way Jesus has shown us how to live:

1. in loving every person despite their skin color
2. in loving every person despite what country they were born into
3. in loving every person despite what faith they were raised up in
4. in loving every person despite whether they are sinners or saints
5. in loving every person despite their intelligence levels
6. in loving every person despite their level of wealth, rich, middle class or poor
7. in loving every person despite of who they are to us, whether they are family or they are our enemies

So, Christ needs you to do his work in the world where he placed you, using your strengths and gifts to help build up the lives of the people that live near you each day. We have to allow Jesus to take us out of the dark pantry and plant us in the soil out in the daylight, so that we can be born again into a new life, living a life freed from those sins and mistakes that have so long controlled our lives. On the other hand, if we choose to remain in the darkness, our lives would become useless to God and we would then die apart from that new life.

I grew up in a family with two brothers and four sisters on a farm in Illinois. Each one of us shared the same parents, the same aunts and uncles, the same cousins. We learned our values for hard work by living/working /playing on the farm. We all went to the same grade and high school. Like all families we shared many good family times and we also experienced the pains and worry of disease. My siblings and I share many of the same experiences, but each one of us is a totally different individual from our other siblings. What made us so different?

1. Our interests in the world
2. Our faith in God
3. Our choice of spouse
4. The children born to that love
5. Our love for serving our country
6. Our love for serving our family
7. Our willingness to be active in our neighborhoods
8. Our love for music
9. Our participation in sports
10. Our intelligence levels
11. Our interest in different subjects of knowledge
12. Our ability to make friends

With these many differences we each became seven totally different individuals because of those different types of experiences, just look at the differences between us seven siblings:

1. Religion: Catholic, Baptist, Lutheran, Congregational
2. Politics: Republican and Democrat
3. Job Choices: Nurse, agriculture salesman, insurance industry, teacher, business owner
4. Four mothers and two fathers, I have no children
5. Education: Associate / Bachelors / Master's degree
6. Family is very important to all
7. Neighbors and Community service very important to all
8. We all have a deep love for our country
9. Health: we all face possible major health concerns for our lives: both our parents and grandparents all died fairly young from either cancer or heart disease, diabetes also runs in the family, asthma also runs in the

family and my own inherited neurological disease runs
in the family as well

Of the two brothers who grew up in a family where their
parents taught them how to steal and take part in the rougher
aspects of life, one son ended up in jail while the other son
turned away from his family's kind of life and went on to lead
a good and holy life. Why the difference? Each child was given
different gifts and each made a choice in how they chose to
live in the world. It is the same for every child born into this
world; we all are given to the world for a specific purpose. We
each are placed in a specific place in the world, to a specific
set of parents, born to a specific race, born into a certain level
of poverty or wealth. Each of us is given specific gifts in which
we can excel at in our lives, whether we use these gifts becomes
our choice.

My father loved farming the land, my mother loved working
with people as a nurse, and they both loved caring for their
family. Both of my parents were shaped by their difficult
childhoods, my dad lived through the great depression and
all its many struggles, while my mom grew up in Germany
amidst a great depression and deep political turmoil. Mom
and Dad both experienced the war from different points of
view: 1) my dad as a soldier fighting in France, Belgium and
Germany 2) my mom as a civilian living amidst a frightening
war, especially while living in Berlin during the many bombing
raids. Both parents were greatly changed by their experiences
in war, for their experiences helped shape the kind of man or
woman God called them to be in life.

The fears my parents faced during World War II gave them
each a strength that helped them through the other hard times in
life. My mother struggled with cancer for many years, while my
dad dealt with problems with his heart for several years as well.
My dad's faith was always very private, he didn't like church
because he had seen too many men and women who professed
to be Christians, who were the pillars of the community, but

these "pillars" also did not lead very moral lives, or in the way they treated other people in the community the other six days of the week. I know my dad prayed hard during the hard times, but he mostly lived out his faith by his love and service to his family, to his friends, to his community and to his country. My dad's father and grandfather felt the same way about Church— full of Christians who were hypocrites during the rest of the week. While my mother's faith was much stronger and more vocal, prayer was very important to her, as was her love for the Sacraments of the Catholic Church; she also lived her life in service to her family, to her friends, to her community, and to her new country.

Let us now look at the larger world and recognize the vast differences found within the people of our world. Our world has over seven billion people living today, all born because of our God's love for each one of us, living in one hundred ninety two separate countries in the world.

1. Wealth: Three and one-half billion people in extreme poverty, living on less than three dollars a day
   a. About sixty-eight million people out of seven billion people hold about ninety percent of all the money in the world, while the rest fall in between the two groups.[26]
2. Gender: male and female
3. Basic race colors: white, black, Asian, Indian, Hispanic, and many other variations
4. Politics: 1) Democracy 2) Monarchy 3) Dictatorship 4) Republic 5) Transitional
5. Education: literate or illiterate
6. Reading interests: science, history, politics, mystery, fiction, non-fiction, religion, math, autobiographies, comics, sports, finance, romance, horror, etc.

---

[26] *data taken from(http://en.wikipedia.org/wiki/*
Demographics_of_the_world)

7. IQ levels: Profoundly retarded to super genius
8. Schools: Grade school, High School, Associate's Degree, Bachelor's Degree, Master's Degree, or Doctorate's Degree, no education, or self taught, special education classes
9. Religious:
    a. Christianity: Catholic Church, Greek Orthodox Catholic Church and 300 different Catholic Churches, and over 30,000 different Protestant denominations, 2.1 billion Christians
    b. Islam: 1.2 billion people
    c. Judaism: 15 million
    d. Hindu: 850 million
    e. Buddhism: 330 million
    f. Non-religious: 700 million
    g. Atheism: 200 million[27]
10. Life expectancy: from 40 years old on up to up to 80 plus years
11. Living in city/country:
    a. city: over 3 billion people
    b. country: over 3 billion people[28]
12. Jobs: we have 4.2 trillion jobs in the world; there are literally thousands of different kinds of jobs across the world.[29]
13. Percentage of land devoted to farming:
    a. arable land comprises 10% of the total
    b. permanent crops area 1%
    c. meadows and pastures, are 24%
    d. forest and woodland is 31%

---

[27]   *data taken from (http://en.wikipedia.org/wiki/Demographics_of_the_world)*

[28]   *data taken from (http://en.wikipedia.org/wiki/Demographics_of_the_world)*

[29]   *data taken from (http://en.wikipedia.org/wiki/World_economy)*

e. the remaining 34% is land surface that supports little or no vegetation: Antarctica, deserts, mine sites, urban areas[30]

14. Recreation: sports, gambling, movies, exercise, fishing, hunting, radio, television, drinking alcohol, taking drugs, pornography.

   a. average person drinks in USA about 2 gallons of alcohol [31]

   b. illegal drugs, Americans buy over 60 billion dollars worth of drugs

   c. gambling: 482 billion is spent on legal gambling, many billion more dollars are spent on illegal gambling[32]

   d. fast food, we spend over 110 billion dollars[33]

   e. cigarettes, we spend over 82 billion dollars [34]

   f. video gaming over 5 billion dollars [35]

   g. movies: well over 10 billion dollars[36]

   h. pornography: 3.8 billion dollars[37]

---

[30]   data taken from (http://en.wikipedia.org/wiki/Arable_land)

[31]   data taken from (http://en.wikipedia.org/wiki/Beer_in_the_United_States)

[32]   data taken from (http://en.wikipedia.org/wiki/Illegal_drug_trade)

[33]   data taken from (http://en.wikipedia.org/wiki/Fast_food_restaurant#Consumer_spending)

[34]   data taken from (http://en.wikipedia.org/wiki/Comprehensive_Smoking_Education_Act)

[35]   data taken from (http://en.wikipedia.org/wiki/Video_gaming_in_the_United_States)

[36]   data taken from (http://en.wikipedia.org/wiki/Cinema_of_the_United_States)

[37]   data taken from (http://en.wikipedia.org/wiki/Pornography_in_the_United_States)

15. Crime levels: over 10 million people in the world are in jail today, with the greatest number being in the USA, well over 2.5 million people[38]

16. Sizes of Armed Services: over 97,664,000 men/women in armed services / reserves/paramilitary in 168 countries. How much money do we spend on military:
   a. USA – 692 billion annually
   b. China – 80.6 billion annually
   c. France – 65 billion
   d. UK – 65 billion
   e. Russia –58 billion
   f. Germany – 46 billion
   g. Japan – 46 billion
   h. Italy – 40 billion
   i. Saudi Arabia--38 billion
   j. India – 30 billion[39]

17. USA uses each year 25% of the world's resources with a population of only 5 % of the whole world's total population, eating over 10% of all food produced in the world.[40]

18. There are perhaps hundreds of other things that can separate us and make us different from other people:
   a. sexuality
   b. skin color
   c. hair color
   d. eye color
   e. married /single/children
   f. choice of music
   g. the clothes you wear
   h. your health

---

[38]   *data taken from (http://en.wikipedia.org/wiki/United_States)*

[39]   *data taken from (http://en.wikipedia.org/wiki/ List_of_countries_by_military_expenditures)*

[40]   *data taken from (http://en.wikipedia.org/wiki/Natural_resource_economics)*

i. physical diseases
j. mental diseases
k. moral / immoral choices
l. family structure or lack of in home
m. favorite tastes of food
n. physical height
o. weight sizes
p. personality types
q. blood type

Is it any wonder there is so much division and struggle in the world, we see it every day in the newspapers all across the world, in our nation, in our local towns and cities. Our papers are filled with tragedy after tragedy: war, murder, robberies, suicides, drug abuse, homeless people, unemployment, people with no health insurance, anger over how our government is run, kidnappings, abortions, car accidents, divorce, rape and molestation victims, stories of people dying from cancer, the list goes on and on. Our television shows are often filled with violence, each day; we see dozens of murders and many other acts of violence on our television sets, so much so that we no longer are bothered by those people dying on our screens. The video game industry has also made billions of dollars on games that promote the killing of others, hurting others, stealing and lying. Even some of our music today reflects many of the same immoral aspects of our culture.

The Lord is telling us how we are known by God in this scripture: *"Before I formed you in the womb I knew you, before you were born I dedicated you, a prophet to the nations I appointed you."*[41] Are we as humans really that different from the next person? First off, each and every person born into this world knew God before we were born; each one of us is infused with the breath of God, given a soul which separates us from the animals. We all are made by God and placed in the world

---

[41] *Jer.1:5,NAB*

for a specific purpose, which means that every person in God's view has value to Him, so much so that he gave to the world His only son Jesus Christ, dying on the cross for everyone's sins and choices for life.

Scientists say today, that every person ever born is .9975 % alike genetically, which means that we are way more alike than we are different. We have the same amount of bones, the same body organs, the same numbers of fingers and toes, the same system of veins and arteries with a heart as our pump. Each of our bodies is a miracle of nature, a perfect system dependent upon the functioning of the brain. Every child is formed within their mother's womb after being conceived when the egg and sperm unite. The .005% differences are instances due to genetic flaws or environmental effects that some children are born with a physical or mental disability. I was born with an average IQ range, while Einstein was born with a super genius IQ level. I worked with children who have fairly low IQ's, those at the bottom of the intelligence spectrum. I currently have what is called a moderate physical disability, while Steven the child I held in college had a severe physical disability that has kept him confined to a wheelchair and dependent upon others for all of his needs.

Why is one person born into abject poverty, while another is born into a wealthy family? Or, why is one child born with good health and the next is born with a physical or mental disability? Or, why is one child born into a family who is Muslim and the next child is born into a family that is Christian? Or, why is one child born in Africa and another child is born in England? I see all these things as a mystery coming from God, not to remain ignorant of the mystery, but this questioning of these mysteries helps us to search out God, it becomes for us an opportunity for developing a deeper relationship with God.

Go back to the time you first met your first love or spouse. Didn't you have a sense of mystery or nervousness around this person? Didn't you want to get to know this person at a deeper level, so you might have spent hours talking to that person, in getting to know that person at those deep spiritual and intellectual levels? That is how God uses all the mysteries found within the world, for they catch our eyes and make us wonder about the big things about life, and so we will often make that effort and spend more time with God and listen to what He has to say to us about the world.

What parent wouldn't grieve over a child that was just convicted over a major crime like murder? In most cases these parent's hearts are broken because of what their child now has to face far into the future. I know there are some parents who believe that they are the cause of their child's crime, in some cases it might be true, but more than likely it is not the parent's fault. We must know that God grieves for those people that are lost in their lives of sin, and that He rejoices when a person accepts the Lord's grace and gives their sins back to God, scriptures says the angels and God rejoice when lives are brought back home to heaven.

No matter what the circumstance of our lives, the love and presence of God remains in the world and hopefully will remain within each of our lives. It becomes for us a matter of choosing the life we are presently living, or the new life being offered to us by Jesus from the cross. I know I haven't always thought about God's mysteries in my life, it first started with the onset of my physical health problems during my teen years and especially when I was confined to my wheelchair during my early twenties. So as a young man my attention wasn't always on building a relationship with God, but was mostly focused on just growing up as a young man, earning my high school diploma, being responsible for my own actions, working at a job that would support my goals: car, dating, schooling, clothes, etc.

It started out as a question, "Why me Lord, why must I struggle with this disease?" Why do I have to use a wheelchair? Why did I have to lose all those things I truly loved in life as a child, like, running races, climbing trees, walking up and down hills, playing basketball, riding a bike? I left college because I had grown too weak to be able to walk to my classes. In my

eyes I came home as a failure from college, having to become
dependent upon my parents for my very survival:

1. I was protected by their shelter that they paid for with
   the money they earned.
2. I was given their food to eat.
3. I wore the clothes they bought, and the clothes they
   washed for me.
4. I used their money in paying for my insurance—money
   which paid for my doctor's bills.
5. I used their physical strength for getting me up and
   down a flight of stairs while sitting in a wheelchair.
6. I accepted their love for me each day; it gave me the
   strength to face another day in the world.
7. I accepted the faith that my mother gave us as kids—in
   attending Mass each Sunday, in receiving the Lord's
   Sacraments, especially the Eucharist.

At my weakest I probably slept up to twenty hours a day,
some of it was probably due to depression, but mostly it was
because my disease left me little strength. I remember crying
myself to sleep on some nights, begging God to let me die
during the night, or that He would give me some hope to make it
through another day. In asking the above question and seeking
God's will in my life, God gave me the desire to seek His
son Jesus out in the world, in looking for an answer to this
great question. So I began a journey I had called in the past,
"my search for the truth." I read many books in searching
for Jesus, and here are some topics of the books I read: the
Bible, Catholic Church, liturgy, Church history, Saints, prayer,
different Protestant beliefs, Islam, Judaism, Hinduism, Taoism,
reincarnation and ancient histories of the world.

Throughout these readings I had searched for the truth about
where Jesus could be found within our world, but I learned
from my readings that all truth about Jesus must begin from
within our very own being; that we must look within our soul

and meet Jesus face-to-face. Remember the question I asked God; about why I was called to live my life with such a struggle. Christ told me this in response, "Why not you? What makes you any different from all those folks with cancer; or those folks suffering from starvation or all the other people suffering within our world? This personal struggle you are facing will greatly bless your life, in ways you cannot ever imagine, or you can remain mired by this struggle and learn nothing about life or your faith." I can truly say that this struggle with my disease has truly shaped my whole life and it has blessed my life immeasurably.

When I broke my femur bone in 2010, I was forced back into the wheelchair; my whole life was changed once again. I was now isolated from the children I had loved and served my whole life. I was taken out of a position that had defined my life for the last twenty five years. Again I was forced to rely on my wife or friends for specific types of help and it humbles me greatly to be so dependent upon others. In time I will see this current struggle as another great blessing in my life, but the struggle remains even today, because this is what makes us human, living life amidst pain and anguish for what the future and God may bring to us.

In 1990, after I left the seminary, I wanted to be the one in charge of my future, working and providing for my needs each day. I still struggle with this need to be as independent as I can be in life. I have always had a fatalistic view for living into my senior years, thinking that because of my family's history with both my grandparents and parents who all died at a very young age; then I too would die fairly young as well. I knew from a young age that the natural progression of my Charcot-Marie-Tooth disease would gradually weaken my arms and legs, and I would end up back in the wheelchair. It has been hard to experience again the gradual loss of physical strength and seeing my world grow smaller each day.

It may seem that I have an extreme dislike for the wheelchair and that I think of it as a death sentence for my life. Initially

I saw the wheelchair as a sign that first symbolized my death as a student in college—it took me away from the life "I" had planned for my future and it brought me back to where I was once again dependent upon my parent's love. And out of this great struggle in my youth I sought out and was given a closer relationship with Jesus Christ, and together we worked towards a whole new kind of a future for me to follow in my life—my life as special education teacher serving those precious children given by God for the world, and I was able to do this job for twenty-six years, and I loved every moment I had within the classroom—for I knew this is where I was always meant to be.

Have you ever walked along a pathway that was sloping upwards, a pathway you had never been on before, you can see the top of the path a long way off, you look ahead and wonder what lies ahead for you on this journey? Each one of our lives has periods where we can see what lies ahead of us, but we each can't see beyond the horizon at the top of this hill until we are on top of this part of the pathway. Let me give an example, there is a young couple expecting their first child, they are walking on a path just like their parents had once taken, knowing that in about eight months or so, there will be a child born to them, so the young couple would begin to prepare a room for their new baby. The young mother does everything she can to ensure the baby is growing healthy inside her. Then one day the couple reached the top of the hill and the baby is born and a new pathway is laid out before them, those parents were given a child far different than what they expected, not a normal healthy child, but instead their child was born with a severe physical and/or mental disability. The pathway before them now is one they could never have expected or imagined. I have worked with parents who had a child that was born with a severe disability, and I have witnessed the depth of their love for their most special child, a love that is really no different than the one they have shown their other "normal" children, but they are following a much different kind of pathway than a parent of a normal child, make no mistake about it.

My whole purpose in writing this chapter on the "World and Our Place in It," is because each person often lives out their lives shaped by their family's love and values, and their individual life situations and their choices throughout their lives. Each person is given many gifts and strengths in which shape and mold their lives, plus each one of us is shaped by our own mistakes and choices in life as well. All of these facets become the rings or layers that surround our basic humanness, which for mankind is our soul; it is this breath from God that separates us from the animals. Because of our fallen nature, we struggle between living a Godly life through Christ and living our life apart from Christ.

"In order that you may know how to arm yourself against this vice, we offer the following considerations. Consider how many labors Christ endured for you from the beginning until the end of His life. Consider how he passed many nights without sleep, praying for you, how he was constantly traveling across Galilee, preaching and healing people. Consider that He was always occupied with the things that pertain to your salvation and how he carried the heavy weight of the cross upon His holy shoulder, already weary from past labors. If the Lord of such great majesty labored so strenuously for your salvation, how much reason you have to work for it also."[42]

"If at times we find that we are overwhelmed by many labors, let us remember that it is through many tribulations that we must enter the kingdom of God, and that only he is crowned who strives to make it through to another day. And if it seems to you that you have already worked and struggled enough, remember the

---

[42] *P.172, excerpt used from "Summa of the Christian Life," vol. 2, Tan Books, Charlotte, NC, used with permission, (www.tanbooks.com)*

words of scripture: 'He that shall persevere unto the end, he shall be saved.' Without perseverance, efforts will not bear fruit; there will be no reward for labors; the runner in the race will not achieve victory. Let us never cease to do penance and to carry our cross in imitation of Christ. Nor should we be dismayed at the difficulties involved in our struggles and labors. God sees our combats, He will come to our aid when we are weakened and He will crown us when we are victorious.'[43]

We have to give to Jesus our gifts and knowledge, and we have to be willing to allow Jesus to take out of our lives those thoughts and actions that don't help build up the kingdom of God, taking away those things that keep us separate from other people. We have to view each person as a gift from heaven, which of course is true. We have to be willing to work and serve the Lord our whole lives, through prayer, through his Church, in knowing him in the scripture, and in service to his people. Following Christ is not an easy pathway and it requires our every effort and thought, we need to keep our eyes focused on Christ, but the journey is not a lonely one, for Christ is at our side, he is showing us the way to his Father, his Holy Spirit is a great teacher and counselor who teaches us about Jesus, and the Catholic Church is the church established by Jesus, to be an instrument of God's grace in the world.

---

[43]   *p.173, 174, excerpt used from "Summa of the Christian Life," vol. 2, Tan Books, Charlotte, NC, used with permission, (www.tanbooks.com)*

CHAPTER 4

WHAT DO YOU BELIEVE IN?

This is perhaps the hardest question anyone of us will have to face in our relationship with Christ in his world. Am I doing what God is expecting of me? Am I living my faith through Jesus Christ, allowing his words to be spoken through my mouth or allowing his work to be completed through my daily actions? Do we love those people Christ has placed into our lives? What is it that we are doing which keeps us so busy in our lives? Is it God's work, or is it "my" work?

These are some of the questions that came out of my prayers as I prepared for this chapter. What do I believe in? This question has pierced my heart and forced me to look at my own belief systems. Our belief systems control every aspect of our lives. They control the types of jobs we choose, or the types of foods we like to eat. All of our thoughts and actions will always reflect the systems from which we were raised in. These belief systems will change as we begin to live life on our own. Some of these belief systems we will keep and some others we will change to meet our present understandings. Our every action or inaction in life is based on these belief systems as well, and sometimes several of these belief systems will keep us from becoming a part of Christ. So take some time today and search within your own heart and discover those truths from which you live out your life.

1. Are you happy or sad?
2. Are you content with your life?
3. Are you confused or lonely?
4. Is life exciting for you?
5. Or, does your life suck out your spirit?

6. Are you ever satisfied with yourself?
7. Do you put blame on others for your inactions?
8. Are you always tired and feeling out of control?
9. Do you like to complain about the hardness that life often gives to us?
10. Who do you blame for our world's problems?
11. Who do you blame for your own problems?

I think by now that you realize that we can keep on asking these types of questions for many more pages. Our task now is to face each of the questions before us and recognize how these attitudes and actions have shaped and propelled us forward in life. The Apostle Paul also struggled with these same types of questions within his own life and he has shared his thoughts in the letters he wrote to the various churches he founded. It is in answering these types of questions that we will come to recognize their impact on our life with Christ.

"Now if I do what I do not want, I concur that the law is good. So now it is no longer I who do it, but sin that dwells in me. For I know that good does not dwell in me, that is my flesh. The willing is really at hand, but the doing the good is not. For I do not the good I want, but I do the evil I do not want. Now if I do what I do not want, it is no longer I who do it, but sin that dwells in me. So, then, I discover the principle that when I want to do right, evil is at hand. For I take delight in the law of God, in my inner self, but I see in my members another principle at war with the law of my mind, taking me captive to the law of sin that dwells in my members. Miserable one that I am! Who will deliver me from this mortal body?"[44]

---

[44]   *Rom.7:16-24, NAB*

This scripture explains to us the powers that sin often has over our lives. When these sins or ways of life are tied so closely to our belief systems they become hidden from our awareness. We have placed so much value on how we have chosen to live out our own lives that we have failed to bring to Jesus these parts of our lives. Is this the way Christ wants us to live? Is the way we are living right now as a part of Christ's plan, or are we just living out our lives as we see fit? Christ is our only hope for breaking away from our sinful nature. Christ has given us the opportunity to bring to him all aspects of our lives. Christ wants to break us free of these bonds of slavery in order to live a life fully in him. His death on the cross is our key to this great grace within our lives, turning away from those actions that enslave us to our past and the freedom to choose a whole new way of life.

"That is not how you learned Christ, assuming that you have heard of him and were taught in him, as truth is in Jesus, that you should put away the old self of your former way of life, corrupted through deceitful desires, and be renewed in the spirit of your minds, and put on the new self, created in God's way in righteousness and holiness of truth. Therefore, putting away falsehood, speak the truth, each one to his neighbor, for we are members one of another."[45]

God gives each one of us the freedom to choose how we live out our lives; for He will not force us to love Him or His son Jesus. The responsibility for choosing the way of our life lies within us. Do we accept Christ's sovereignty over our lives, or will we continue to function out of our old belief systems? Not all belief systems are wrong or sinful. Many of them can be very pleasing and holy to God. Our danger lies in not being able to recognize the sins within these belief systems.

---

[45] *Eph.4:20-25,NAB*

"Belief is a state of the mind, treated in various academic disciplines, especially philosophy and psychology, as well as traditional culture, in which a subject roughly regards a thing to be true."[46]

When we look upon our beliefs as truthful and good for our lives; we are often blinded to their effects on the world Christ has placed us in. If our actions are of Christ they will always bear fruit in God's kingdom. If our actions are not of Christ, they will always bring some level of harm into our world. Many of our actions will reflect from those experiences and people that are a part of our lives. Let me now list some types of beliefs in which we may or may not live out our lives in. Please take some time and evaluate each of these areas within your life. Once you pray over these areas then go to Jesus and ask him to shed his light upon each of these areas within your life:

1. Income levels:
   a. wealthy
   b. middle class
   c. poor
2. Our choice for an occupation will often reflect the types of jobs our parents worked at. They are also shaped by our personality and educational abilities. Our job choice will reflect the values of both our family and what society is impressed with. Our choice is also dependent upon our ability to afford a higher education.
3. Type of family structure:
   a. healthy family life with a secure loving family
   b. healthy family life with secure loving divorced parents
   c. a family that is unstable and always fighting
   d. a family swamped with many burdens, working several jobs

---

46   *Data taken from (http://en.wikipedia.org/wiki/Belief)*

e. you come from a family where your parents are addicted to alcohol or drugs
f. perhaps we live with parents who are self serving and materialistic
g. perhaps our parents were so busy with their jobs they didn't have the time to raise their own children.
h. perhaps the children grew up in day care or a boarding school. These environments can also be very nourishing and loving, or they can be very confusing for a child. The parents can be very loving towards their children, or perhaps they really did not want to take the time to raise their children.

4. Family's values are another area of deep impact on our lives.
   a. sense of family unity
   b. helping other people
   c. serving your community
   d. educational
   e. religious background
   f. prayer life
   g. political beliefs
   h. work ethic
   i. patriotism
   j. ethnic background
   k. being able to express love
   l. parent's verbal or physically abusive
   m. incest
   n. drug and alcohol abuse
   o. racism
   p. hatred for other people
   q. parent's involved with adultery
   r. laziness
   s. parents were real clean people
   t. parents were very dirty people
   u. cultural values
   v. religious beliefs

5. Political systems:
   a. Democrat
   b. Republican
   c. Independent
   d. Socialist
   e. Communist
   f. Progressive
6. National political systems:
   a. Democracy
   b. Socialist
   c. Communist
   d. Republic
   e. Dictatorship
   f. Monarchy
7. Economic system:
   a. capitalist
   b. communist
8. Cultural heritage:
   a. white - European descent
   b. black - Africa descent
   c. native American Indian
   d. Asian descent
   e. Hispanic
9. Educational background:
   a. illiterate
   b. grade school level
   c. high school diploma
   d. bachelor's degree
   e. master's degree
   f. doctorate
10. Intelligence levels:
    a. gifted
    b. normal intelligence
    c. learning disabled
    d. mentally disabled
11. Health of our body:

 a. great health
 b. cancer
 c. heart problems
 d. diabetes
 e. physically handicapped
 f. disabled from a gunshot
 g. disabled from a car accident or other injury
 h. burn victim
 i. blind
 j. hearing impaired
 k. mentally disabled
 l. behavior disordered
 m. birth defects
 n. childhood diseases
 o. mental disease
12. Personal addictions:
 a. alcohol
 b. cigarettes
 c. illegal drugs
 d. lying
 e. stealing
 f. cussing
 g. sexual
 h. gambling
 i. pornography
 j. eating disorders
 k. stealing
13. Religious background:
 a. Christian: Catholic, Protestant, non-denominational
 b. Mormon
 c. Islam
 d. Judaism
 e. Moslem
 f. Buddhism
 g. New Age
 h. Agnostic

14. Views on the way we approach our God and our relationships with people from other religious backgrounds
15. Personality types:
    a. quiet
    b. shy
    c. thoughtful
    d. easy going
    e. soft spoken
    f. telling others what they think
    g. bossy
    h. out-going
    i. gregarious
16. Our ability to relate with other people, our family, and our friends is greatly dependent upon our type of personality and those experiences with our family/friends/co-workers.
17. Our ability to think through all of our life's actions and decisions are dependent upon all the above belief systems, for they are all inter-related and co-dependent upon one another.

Where does Jesus fit into each of these aspects of our lives? Only you can answer these questions for yourself. The beliefs from which we function are often at odds with the life that Jesus is calling us into. How we think and act towards other people is also a reflection of our experiences in relating to the people within our life. We need to follow Jesus and accept his grace and teachings in our lives. Our every action and every word should reflect the truths of Jesus love in our everyday world. But doing what Christ asks of us can be very hard and uncomfortable for us at times.

His disciples often found it hard to understand Jesus' message, for his words cut to the heart of who they were as individuals. Against the light of Christ we are now able to recognize within ourselves those beliefs that do not belong to

God. Only when we can see our beliefs through God's eyes can we see their impact on our lives and on the lives of the people we live with each day. When we recognize this belief's impact on our lives we can now decide to offer this action over to Jesus. Each moment of the day Jesus is calling for us to live in him, to share in his unconditional love for all people. Christ is calling us to be a people of compassion and one that is always able to forgive others of their sins and actions. The decision is ours to make. Do we accept Christ fully into our lives, or do we chase after our own gods of this world?

CHAPTER 5

2ND CHANCES

"The chief priests and the elders persuaded the crowds to ask for Barabbas but to destroy Jesus. The governor said to them in reply, 'Which of the two do you want me to release to you?' They answered, 'Barabbas!' Pilate said to them, 'Then what shall I do with Jesus called Messiah?' They all said, 'Let him be crucified!' But he said, 'Why? What evil has he done?' They only shouted the louder, 'Let him be crucified!' When Pilate saw that he was not succeeding at all, but that a riot was breaking out instead, he took water and washed his hands in the sight of the crowd, saying, 'I am innocent of this man's blood. Look to it yourselves.' And the whole people said in reply, 'His blood be upon us and upon our children.' Then he released Barabbas to them, but after he had Jesus scourged, he handed him over to be crucified."[47]

Or!

"Now one of the criminals hanging there reviled Jesus, saying, 'Are you not the Messiah? Save yourself and us.' The other, however, rebuking him, said in reply, 'Have you no fear of God, for you are subject to the same condemnation? And indeed, we have been condemned justly; for the sentence we received corresponds to our crimes, but this man has done nothing criminal.' Then he said, 'Jesus, remember me when you come into your

---

[47]   *Matt.27:20-26,NAB*

*kingdom.' He replied to him, 'Amen, I say to you, today
you will be with me in Paradise.'"[48]*

Which of the two men in the scriptures above received a
2nd chance, Barabbas or the second thief hanging on a cross?
Barabbas got a 2nd chance for life amongst his people, while
the second thief died on the cross and was brought home into
Paradise with Jesus. In reality both men received a 2nd chance
for a new view towards life, one while still living on earth; and
the other's will be from heaven. I have often wondered how
Barabbas lived his life after being let go by Pontius Pilate. Did
he now live a moral life devoted to God? Barabbas was truly
given a 2nd chance for a new beginning, and in many ways he
represents each one of us, because we all are sinners and in
some small way we know deep down that we are undeserving
of this great chance given to us by Jesus.

The second thief recognized his own evil before Jesus as he
hung from his own cross; the second thief basically confessed
his sins to Jesus. The second thief recognized that Jesus was
truly innocent of any sin, and that he didn't deserve to die like
this on the cross. Surely this man knew the gravity of his own
sins and the price that needed to be paid by him in doing those
crimes, it is obvious that this second thief had a change of heart,
and he did show remorse for those sins, and Jesus forgave him
from his own cross. We have to believe that if Jesus can change
these two men's lives; then he can change our own.

Several times in a bible study my friends and I would
like to tackle several "what if type" questions as a way for
understanding our faith better, for instance, if Hitler confessed
his sins to God or a Priest right before he died, would he be in
heaven? He could have been like the second thief and confessed
his sins with heartfelt emotions, meaning that he truly repented
from the evil he had done within his life. As Christians we have
to believe that Hitler had the potential to be forgiven and to be

---

[48]   *Luke 23:39-43, NAB*

given a new life with God. As a sinner ourselves, we have to believe that every person can be saved by God through Jesus' death on the cross. How else could we find the courage to accept God's will, and then turn our lives over to Jesus—even though we might feel we can never be forgiven for what we have done or said in our lives.

I think because of our own weak human nature, we at times think we have the ability and the right to judge other people for their sins and actions. It was the reason Adam and Eve ate from the tree of knowledge so they can see and know as God does. This one action by Adam and Eve separated mankind from his God, and ever since this one act of disobedience, mankind has been seeking from God this 2nd chance to rebuild their relationship between themselves and their God. Deep down I think we each miss that closeness we once had with our Father in the Garden of Eden. I have learned through experience and from what I have read from the bible that we can't bridge the gulf between us and God through our own efforts. The very fact that we still think this way; only proves that we are still very much like Adam and Eve in that we still believe we can be like God and control our own destiny.

But our world was not made this way, for God made the world and He formed us each from dust, and He breathed His life into our bodies. We have to learn to recognize our place in God's world. God is our creator and Father, Jesus is our Lord and Savior and brother, and we were created for the world that we were placed in, to be a sign of our Father's love. And upon our death, our physical body will return to the dust from which we came, but depending in how we lived and loved in God's world and followed His Son's narrow path, our soul, or God's breath would return to Him in heaven. But if we chose to live our life apart from God then our soul faces a different kind of future, a future that is forever cut off from God.

We don't enter heaven as equals with God or Jesus; we are there to worship and honor God and His Son for all eternity. The 2nd chance we are given today ultimately will bring us to heaven, providing that we assume our place in the world, and accept the will of the Father and live out our lives through Jesus. Jesus instructs us on a truth of God's grace from this scripture: *"Not everyone who says to me, Lord, Lord, will enter the kingdom of heaven, but only he who does the will of my Father who is in heaven."*[49]

In the previous chapters we discussed at length all the differences that separate us as a people living in the world, heaven is not based on skin color, or race, or nationality, or the religion we were born into in this world. We have to realize that God and Jesus knew each one of us in heaven before we were placed in this world, so we know God loves us regardless of all these differences as well. Jesus' death on the cross was for all mankind, not one part, not one color, not one race. His death on the cross, is because of the sins we have all committed against God, can't you hear your own voice yelling in the crowd, crucify him, crucify him. Jesus says that he is the fulfillment of this old covenant, and that a new covenant between heaven and mankind is made and sealed by the blood that he shed on the cross for our sins. We have to see ourselves as a Barabbas who was given a 2nd chance to live his life in a new way, or the second thief who confessed his sins and was able to join Jesus that day in Paradise, otherwise there is no future for us, without God there is no future for us at all.

Barabbas could have returned to his old life, there always was that chance, but I think we all hope that he began a new life following Jesus. I think deep down within our own soul we all believe we have that chance to begin a new life in order to return to that closeness we once had with God before we were placed in the world. If the mother you loved was dying from cancer, we would never pray that our mother not be healed of this cancer, we would want her to be fully restored to our lives. When Jesus healed the paralytic he restored him fully to life physically. When my mother prayed for me I truly believe she

---

49   *Matt.7:21,NAB*

wanted my body to be fully healed, every mother or father would want nothing less for their own child. So, we have to believe that Barabbas was restored to life for a purpose; a purpose that both glorified God and Jesus' ultimate sacrifice from the cross, a cross that rightly belonged to Barabbas in the first place.

2nd Chance: Mary Magdalene

> *"Afterward he journeyed from one town and village to another, preaching and proclaiming the good news of the kingdom of God. Accompanying him were the Twelve Apostles and some women who had been cured of evil spirits and infirmities, Mary, called Magdalene, from whom seven demons had gone out."*[50]

Mary Magdalene is often mentioned as being a close follower of Jesus, travelling within the group of disciples as they travelled around the country, she was there at the cross, as she was also present at his burial, and she was at the tomb the morning of Jesus' resurrection. Mary Magdalene is mentioned more often than some of the other Apostles. Scripture really doesn't say in what way Mary was affected by her seven demons, but we do know how it affected other people Jesus had healed of being possessed. The demon would be totally controlling the person's whole life and every action. In some ways these demons are like a god, where their will is lived out through this one person—often against the will of this person. How these demons enter the person is not known, maybe she willingly invited them into her life, or they forced their presence into Mary's life. From previous scriptures we know that the demons have no power before Jesus, and each of the demons recognized the Lord's sovereignty over their world, and they didn't hesitate in following the Lord's commands when told by Jesus to leave

---

[50]   *Luke 8:1-2, NAB*

Mary Magdalene. These seven demons must have impacted her life greatly in many ways, and when she was given this 2nd chance for a new future, she became one of Jesus' most ardent of followers.

Why is it that all these demons can follow the Lord's will instantly, and many Christians refuse to follow every aspect of the Lord's will for their own lives? Why do we always choose the actions we like? Our inclination towards sin is the result of man's fall in the Garden of Eden, so now we are more inclined to sin and turn away from God because of our weak human nature, even some of the angels in heaven turned their backs on God. It might seem that we are like Mary Magdalene as well, for our sins often have a certain control over our lives in much the same way as the demons controlled Mary's whole life. But God is telling us that we must think differently, we do have power over these sins, for our soul recognizes through Jesus that these same sins truly don't have the power we give them in our lives, but these sins would disappear if we placed our trust in God's will. The power we have available to us can only come from our Father through His son Jesus.

Mary's freedom didn't begin because she chose a different life; it changed because God willed it through Jesus that she should begin a new and different life through His son. What role do we have in this process for achieving a new life in God? We do have a choice in this you know, we can choose to accept the will of God through Jesus and be changed by this grace, or we can continue to live out our lives apart from God. Our world is filled with people in need of 2nd chances, so how do we get people to open their eyes and open their spirit to the grace given to us by God through His son Jesus Christ? God's will, man does God's will.

2nd Chance: Cure d' Ars, France

"Oh, my friends,' he said, I have not been long in Ars, but I have watched you closely. I see how you live. When

Sunday comes, you go to the fields or to the cabarets. Back and forth you go in front of the church, but many of you do not stop or think to pay a visit to God. My friends, I know what you are thinking too. Of course, M'sieur Cure is a priest; of course he disapproves of the way we live. No my friends, it is not disapproval I feel for you, I feel sorry for you. Why do I feel sorry for you?

Because, my friends, I know that you are throwing away the only thing that really counts Jean Marie was crying harder, what you are throwing away my friends, as if you didn't know. You are throwing away the chance of heaven! And what is heaven, my friends? You know that too, heaven is where one sees God face to face. Think my friends, to see God, what overwhelming happiness you will have."

"But is it not difficult to get to heaven? No my friends, you can go to heaven by keeping a simple little rule. Do only those things that are pleasing to God! Think, my friends. God offers you so much and asks so little, he asks that you live by that one simple rule."⁵¹

The Cure' of Ars has always been one of my favorite saints; he grew up as a farmer helping his father with all the various chores around the farm. Jean Vianney's mother was a holy woman, whose faith encouraged her son to grow in his own faith. Both parents were very kind and generous by their actions to those who were starving and in need of help, they took in priests who feared for their lives from a government who wanted them dead. Although Jean's father was not very spiritual, but he always did what was right for his family. Jean's parents reminded me of my own parents in the way they lived out their

---

⁵¹   *p.28, excerpt used from "The Cure of Ars: The Priest Who Out-Talked the Devil," by Milton Lomask, Ignatius Press, 1958, used with permission, (http://www.ignatius.com)*

lives. Jean always had a hard time learning higher concepts, but his greatest difficulty was in being able to learn and speak in Latin, it was the primary roadblock that prevented him from becoming a priest. It took another priest who recognized Jean's spirituality and was willing to discuss with the Bishop as to why Jean would make a good priest despite some of his learning weaknesses. Both parents sacrificed much for their son, for they knew that Jean had the potential for truly making a difference in the world they lived.

The Cure' of Ars was truly a man sent by God into that small corner of France, to a place that had lost its faith due to neglect and to a world that had forgotten God because of the other smaller gods they followed. Our world is filled with places that has also forgotten God, and throughout time God has raised up people and placed them in specific areas of the world, people like the Cure of Ars, St Francis of Assisi, St. Padre Pio, St. Catherine of Siena, Mother Theresa of Calcutta, Pope John Paul II and many, many others. Throughout the whole of history; God has made the greatest impact on a region of the world through the people He called up to serve and minister to the people, doing not their own will, but the will of our God in heaven. Even today these special people we call saints have the potential for teaching us about God through their efforts and the words they spoke, for God's truth isn't generational, but all truth is eternal and always meant to draw us closer to the Father. God's will, man does God's will.

2nd Chance: God's Covenant

To understand what we lost with original sin, we have to recognize the relationship with God we once had in the Garden of Eden. Prior to eating from the tree of knowledge Adam participated with God in creation, God made an animal or plant, then God brought these things before Adam, and then Adam would give a name to each animal or plant. Adam even participated with God in allowing a woman to be formed from his side. Standing before God naked, tells me also how close God and Adam were in the Garden of Eden, their lives were an open book, and they kept nothing hidden from their God. But when they ate from the tree of knowledge, against God's will, Adam and Eve now saw their own nakedness, so they hid from God behind some trees. The whole relationship with God changed because of Adam and Eve's disobedience. God did not abandon them, for God brought them east from the Garden of Eden where they now had to toil and work the land for their food, tilling the same ground from which they were formed. Scripture after scripture describes the lives of Adam's family throughout history, some stayed true to God's will, but there were many that followed their own will as well. But, as you read through these scriptures you can see God is still very much a part of their lives, so Adam and his family was given a 2nd chance to begin a new life, but with some new added responsibilities. God's will, man does God's will.

2nd Chance: The promise of the Rainbow

The story of Noah is a favorite one for children and many adults. One righteous man was given the task for building a massive boat far in advance of a major world catastrophe, like the great flood. God willed for Noah to build this boat, and Noah did work on this boat even despite all the taunting from his neighbors. Because Noah did as God willed, his family survived the flood. God gave Noah the sign of the rainbow as his promise that never again would He destroy the world through a flood.

"Evan Almighty" is a recent movie that touches upon the theme of Noah, Evan the main character became involved in politics because he wanted to make a difference in his world. God chose Evan to build an Ark, providing all the wood, the blue print for the Ark. God began sending to Evan pairs of two animals to be placed under his care. Evan had many doubts about his role, but he finally began to trust and do as God willed.

His neighbors, friends and wife had a hard time understanding the changes going on in Evan, and it scared them, Evan was surrounded by skeptics, but Evan finished the ark with the help of his sons and the animals that God had sent to him, and on the day of the great flood the boat was surrounded by onlookers, yelling taunts towards Evan, especially when the rain never truly began, but when the lake dam broke and the water came rushing down the valley destroying homes and neighborhoods, the people stopped ridiculing and they ran up the plank into God's Ark where their lives were saved from the flood. One man's faith and hard work saved their lives, and now each person was given an opportunity to change the way they lived in this world. [52]

Sometimes God starts each of us on a path of not our choosing, we see the amount of work that needs to be done in order to achieve this great task for God, like building the ark, so we question God as to why we were given such a task. We can't see where all these efforts take us in our life, our problem is that our vision is too small; we can't see or imagine the future that God has in store for us. Noah couldn't imagine what the great boat would look like, let alone the thousands of hours of hard labor it would take to build the ark. Noah just worked day-by-day, hour-by-hour, step-by-step until the ark was finished, doing the will of God. Even with the boat finished and filled with animals, he still could not understand the magnitude of the flood to come, nor how long it would take for the floods to subside. The world through Noah was given a 2nd chance for life, it doesn't mean that the rebuilding of their world was going to be easy, but it still took great effort and sacrifice, trusting in what God would provide for them far into the future.

There were many people living at the time of Noah, so why did God choose Noah and not some other person to build this

---

[52] *"Evan Almighty," written by Steve Oedekerk, Joel Cohen and Alec Sokolow, Universal Pictures, 2007 (paraphrased from the movie, no direct quotes used)*

ark? Have you ever stood in a room filled with people and you hear a friend calling out your name from across the room, or you are a parent among many parents and yet you can recognize your child's voice calling your name. Why was Noah chosen by God? It was because Noah and the Father had a relationship, they recognized each other's voice and they knew each other. The Father knew that Noah was capable of doing this task physically, and that Noah had the fortitude to see through this great task until the end, even despite what other people thought of him.

The funny thing about history is that usually only the famous people are mentioned in the key parts of history, for we each know the key players of the bible, but what we don't see or hear about are the everyday people. Just look around our country, every football/baseball stadium, bridge or interstate highway is named for a person or a company, what we often forget is that it is the everyday folk who helped build this great stadium or bridge. Solomon is credited with building God's Holy Temple, I am pretty sure he didn't cut any stone or saw down any trees for this Temple, but God used Solomon in a different way. God calls some people to do some extraordinary things, but for the most of us, we just take our place in where God has placed us to love and serve out our lives in following Jesus. What matters is whether each person honors God with their love and their efforts in serving the Lord as we journey through life. I don't have to be this great builder, or great writer, or teacher, or politician to be famous, our greatness doesn't begin with our own actions in life, but our actions shouldn't reflect our image; but our actions should only reflect Jesus back into our world, for only then will our efforts truly honor God.

What about all those people who seem to have been forgotten by God? Our world is filled with them:

1. the homeless man sleeping against a door in the big city
2. a child hunting for items in a garbage dump that she could use to sell and make some money for some food

3. a leper condemned to live out their lives isolated from other people
4. a spouse that just took a beating from her husband for the tenth time
5. a young teenager lost in the world of gang warfare, trying hard each day just to survive
6. an elderly man sitting all alone within his home wondering where everybody went in his life
7. a man who has spent thirty years incarcerated in a maximum security prison for one stupid act as a child.
8. a child refugee from El Salvador stuck at the USA border.
9. I can probably name a hundred more examples of people all around the world, in a world that refuses to see them as a person

What is their worth to God? What role do they have in God's world? I once held a young man the size of an infant, incapable of reading, incapable of writing, incapable of using his hands to work and support himself throughout his life. I grew up in a home where I was expected to work at some task on a farm. This notion for being able to provide for my own needs propelled me out of the wheelchair and into teaching—but this notion has taught us as a society for placing the wrong values on whether a person is worthy of living or not. Hitler believed that so many of the people within Germany were not worthy to be saved by God, so he had them murdered and starved to death in "Death Camps" all across Europe. When we think of the worth of an individual it is always based upon our many belief systems and experiences, and not in what God sees for that person in the world.

The eight forgotten people listed above are given to the world for others to reach out to with all of their love and strength. If the Lord calls me to serve this person, then go I must because it is his will for me. We never heard once in scripture where Jesus turned his eyes away from someone who needed his help—because it was God's will for that man or woman to be healed and forgiven. So, the next time that you "see" someone you think is forgotten by God, then stop and lend them a hand, for it was God who opened your eyes in the first place to this individual. When we stop and serve these folks we are in effect doing the Lord's will, your actions will bring a level of healing into their lives and your actions will point them towards Christ at the cross. Maybe this one act of compassion will help turn their lives around; and when called upon by the Lord one day— then they too can become the instrument of our God's healing touch for another lost soul of the world.

This young man the size of an infant has a purpose that most people don't have the eyes to see in our world. Hitler and many leaders across the world and even in our own country don't recognize the value of each person with a physical, mental or behavioral disability. These most special individuals are one of God's purest souls given to the world for us to learn from and understand about how we are called to live in God's world, with love and a complete trust in His will for us each day.

Who does the world honor more, Noah, or this young man the size of an infant? Of course, most would say Noah because he saved the world. But who does God love more? God doesn't love Noah more, or the young man, he loves them each fully because of whom they were in life, both men lived lives of great faith and both followed the will of God throughout their lives. I spent one hour with this one young man, holding him in my arms and caring for his needs, and I can still remember his name after twenty six years. But I also know that God knows Steven far more intimately than I ever did. This man truly touched my heart in some way that hour, he brought me closer to God, Steven helped open my eyes to new levels of understanding God's will for all life in the world. God's will, man does God's will.

2nd Chances: God giving you a new name

"When Abram was ninety-nine years old, the Lord appeared to him and said: 'I am God the Almighty. Walk in my presence and be blameless. Between you and me I will establish my covenant, and I will multiply you exceedingly.' When Abram prostrated himself, God continued to speak to him: 'My covenant with you is this: you are to become the father of a host of nations. No longer shall you be called Abram; your name shall be Abraham, for I am making you the father of a host of nations. I will render you exceedingly fertile; I will make nations of you; kings shall stem from you. I will maintain my covenant with you and your descendants after you throughout the ages as an everlasting pact, to be your God and the God of your descendants after you. I will give to you and to your descendants after you the land in which you are now staying, the whole land of Canaan, as a permanent possession; and I will be their God.'" [53]

Abram and Sarai lived their lives close to God, but the one thing they wanted was a child, they lost all hope for ever having a child because of their old age, but God gave them a special gift of grace, a new hope for a different kind of future, a future they couldn't grasp or believe in at first. Late in life they were given a 2nd chance; a son was born to them. In Genesis 17, God does something extraordinary for Abram and Sarai; God gave them new names, Abraham and Sarah. It was through Abraham and Sarah that a new covenant was given; where God said He would always be their God for all time, God gave Abraham a promise of a future that few people could ever imagine, a promise of nations, a promise of a kingship and a promise of a future Savior that would come through his line.

---

[53]   *Gen.17:1-8,NAB*

The Covenant is a binding contract between God and His people, God gives and we receive His grace. Is it really that simple, following God? The pattern thus far in history is God acts, the world was created. God acts, Adam and Eve go where God wants them to live. God acts, Noah builds a boat that saves his family. God acts, Abraham and Sarah leave their home and go to where God is preparing their new home. It is God's action and will that transforms our lives into a new creation. We have to accept the will and desire that God has for us in this world, a world formed through His action and grace. The one physical act God demanded of His people was circumcision, an act of obedience to God. God's will, man does God's will, and doing God's will is our act of obedience to God.

2ⁿᵈ Chance: Freedom from Slavery

"After the patriarchs, God formed Israel as his people by freeing them from slavery in Egypt. He established with them the covenant of Mount Sinai and, through Moses, gave them his law so that they would recognize him and serve him as the one living and true God, the provident Father and just judge, and so that they would look for the promised Savior."[54]

One of my favorite memories of Easter is being able to watch the movie the "Ten Commandments." Moses was the instrument in which God freed the people in Egypt, a people who were enslaved by the Egyptian Pharaoh; the people were given a 2ⁿᵈ chance for a new beginning. For most Christians, we know this story by heart, our minds and spirits soar in the telling of this great story. The struggle the people of Israel faced after coming out of Egypt is often compared to the struggle

---

[54] *#62, excerpt used from "Catechism of the Catholic Church," Liberia Editrice Vaticana, Citta del Vaticano, 1997, did not need written approval because I met their guidelines, (http://usccb.org)*

each of us face now as we overcome our ties to Egypt, we haven't learned to trust God's will for our future yet, for we can't see beyond the here and now in our lives, or we are always looking back to our lives in Egypt.

It didn't take long for the people to grumble and moan for a return to a life they had accepted, even despite the labor and punishment they endured from their slavery, so they fashioned themselves a golden calf, a god they could see and worship. This choice, as scripture states so clearly was a deadly one for these people, for they lost their lives through God's judgment. These people refused their 2nd chance for a different kind of future, a future walking with God, and doing the will of God. The people of Israel had become enslaved by their life in Egypt; it is all they ever knew throughout their life. We shouldn't forget the reason why the Israel nation had become slaves in Egypt in the first place, they were there because of their unfaithfulness to God, and it was their punishment for not following God's will.

I have always been amazed at the time it took Moses and the people to travel from Egypt back to the Promised Land, forty years, when at most it would have taken several months to travel at best. I believe this period was filled with blessing after blessing for the people of Israel. This new Covenant was formed at Mt. Sinai where God gave his people a set of Ten Commandments in which the people were expected to live out their lives following. Daily, God willed upon his people, giving them manna from heaven and birds for sustenance, plus water for drink. The people needed to see God's action within their lives over a long time, before they were ready to enter the Promised Land. We must remember that their lives were shaped by generations of unbelief as they served their Egyptian king, so it stands to reason it would take time for the people to learn a new way of life. God's will, man does God's will.

2nd Chance: Will you Build Me a Temple

"When King David was settled in his palace, and the Lord had given him rest from his enemies on every side, he said to Nathan the prophet, 'Here I am living in a house of cedar, while the ark of God dwells in a tent!' Nathan answered the king, 'Go, do whatever you have in mind, for the Lord is with you.' But that night the Lord spoke to Nathan and said: 'go, tell my servant David, Thus says the Lord: Should you build me a house to dwell in?'"[55]

David was man of 2nd chances, he was an on and off kind of man with God, David was a man at a pivotal time in God's world, through David's action as a soldier; a nation was built for the people of Israel. It was through David's obedience to God's will that a new Covenant was given to the nation of Israel; that some day in the future a Savior would be born through David's line. In time God asked David to build a Temple to hold the Ark of the Covenant, a place where God can touch people's lives. But the temple had to wait until David's son Solomon did God's will and built his Temple. This Temple was supposed to be the crowning glory of David's life, but God took this task away from David, because of his disobedience. It might seem at first that God abandoned David, but it was David who took his eyes off of God, for God's covenant remained true to David and the people of Israel, for Jesus was born out of the line of David.

In reading through scripture it is so evident that David was very close to God, and that God had shown favor with him throughout his life, so why would a man like David turn his eyes away from God, especially after all that he had been given? David's story is a common one that transcends time, we see it in every generation, leaders taking advantage of their power, and forgetting their role in God's world. The only answer is that

---

[55]   *2 Sam.7:1-5,NAB*

David was still just a man, fully capable of sin, just like Adam and Eve who ate from the tree of knowledge because they wanted to be like God. Are we really that different from David? Do we always do the will of God within our life? I have not always been close to God, and I have not always used my gifts in the way God intended, but God has never stopped calling my name. God didn't abandon David, nor will he abandon you either, and so must make that choice to entrust to God our very own future, and we must choose to follow Jesus into that future. God's will, man does God's will.

2nd Chance: I am the New Temple

"But this is the covenant which I will make with the house of Israel after those days, says the Lord. I will place my law within them, and write it upon their hearts; I will be their God, and they shall be my people. No longer will they have a need to teach their friends and kinsmen how to know the Lord. All, from least to greatest, shall know me, says the Lord, for I will forgive their evildoing and remember their sin no more."[56]

Wow! Just imagine that each of us right now has the knowledge for knowing God as He has always intended it to be, it is written down in our minds and in our hearts. Every one of us living today has the potential for calling God, our Father. I have good memories of my father, his love for his family, his love for friends and country, or his many hours of work in providing for his family, he was our family's rock. My four sisters, two brothers and I knew we were loved by our parents. My father was very private in some ways; in the way he lived his faith, he never shared his concerns over family finances with us kids, and he rarely spoke of his role in World War II. Dad enjoyed watching sports, and he always stayed up with us

---

[56] *Jer.31:33-34,NAB*

kids on New Year's Eve, playing games with us kids. God is telling us that we can know Him as Jesus knew his Father, or as Mary knew her God, or as St. Peter knew God, or as St. Francis knew God, or as the Cure' of Ars knew God, or as Padre Pio knew God, and certainly way more than we can ever know our own father.

In high school I took two years of Spanish, it was a class I hated because for me the words just didn't click for me, I had a hard time understanding how to convert the words to feminine or masculine tense, let alone forming complete sentences. Greek philosophy in college was another course that numbed my brain, for I could never grasp the different truths being discussed through logic. What God is telling us today is that we each have all the knowledge and understanding of God right now that we need for our journey to heaven. Every person has this knowledge written on their heart and within their mind:

1. people of all faiths
2. people of all colors
3. people of all nations
4. people who are religious, or those that have no interest in God
5. people who are rich or people who are poor
6. people who are healthy, or people who struggle daily with a disability
7. people who are saints, or the sinners of the world
8. people with different intelligence levels

I can't even imagine the totality of God's love, loving each one of us as if we were the most precious gem in the world. God is telling you right now that you are that precious and that His love for us is very real and evident. It is God's love that should compel us to see our life in a whole new way; a life free of those sins that have shaped our lives—for they were washed clean by the blood of Jesus. The knowledge written on our hearts and minds shows us our place in God's world; it says that "God will always be our God," and that "we will always be God's people." So the key for us to understand is that we have to give our sins to God, it doesn't mean we can continue on sinning and still believe we are walking with the Lord. Getting a 2nd chance is all about beginning a new life with God, freed from those very same sins, sins that have impacted our lives and the world we live in. God's will, man does God's will.

My dad was a good man who loved us and raised us to be responsible adults, providing us with a home, food on the table, clothes on our back; we truly knew our dad loved us by his many actions and words shared with us. But, not all children are so fortunate to have a good father, so it may be harder for some to trust in the love and will of the Father. God again is telling us our role in this family, we are to believe in His son Jesus and follow him down this narrow path towards heaven. God acts, God works to bridge the gap between heaven and the world, why can't we see how much God truly loves us yet?

Covenant after covenant, scripture after scripture is showing us how God is so present in our lives and world. It boils down to this, we have God's will and we have our own will that is in a battle for the control over our lives. Eating from the tree of knowledge opened our eyes to the possibilities beyond what God wills for our lives, and most of these possibilities are sinful, or they aren't done for a purpose that glorifies God. Do we accept God as our Father, and Jesus as our Lord and Savior? Or, do we follow our own will and path regardless if it is good for the world or bad for the world? Within our mind and heart lies the truth that God wrote; that "I will be your God, and you will be my people." We have two paths to follow in life: 1] the narrow path of Christ 2] the wide path of the world, one leads to God, and one leads to death and separation from God. On the day of your death what gate do you want to be let into, heaven or hell?

Believing in Jesus is what God wants for each of us today, from a man like Hitler, or a woman like Mother Teresa of Calcutta, or a person like you or I. As a child I believed in

Santa Claus or the Easter Bunny until I reached a certain age. I think for many people they believe in Jesus in much the same way as Santa or the Easter Bunny, they see Jesus as their free ticket to heaven, for Jesus did all the work for dying to each of our sins, perhaps this is why so few people walk the narrow path towards heaven, but travel the wide road of the world. To believe in Jesus requires not only our faith in Jesus and trust for God's will for our life, it requires our effort to do what God wills within the world we now live.

We can just look at how Jesus always followed his Father's will within the world he was born, Jesus' whole life reflected God's will, from the people who joined him as disciples, to his teachings of God's love, to his many healings of people's broken lives, to the daily instruction that the twelve Apostles received about God, to the reason why he formed the Catholic church through Peter and the other Apostles. Believing in Jesus requires a different way we are called to live out our life, it requires communication or prayer with God, plus we must learn to be obedient to God in all things. God is not asking us to give up our will, but to accept his will over our own will in how we live and serve others in our small corner of the world.

Every now and then we hear of a story of a family pet for some reason got stranded several hundred miles from where their master lived, perhaps several states away. I am always dumbstruck that this one cat or dog travelled all those miles just to be home with the people they loved. I think we understand the love of an animal for their master, but how did these family pets find their way back to their master? This cat or dog trusted in the will of their master, their every effort in walking towards home was because their master lived there; it was where this pet knew they belonged. Our journey home to heaven really is no different, the love of our Master compels us to go down that narrow pathway: walking, eating, searching, teaching, working, serving others, or sleeping—putting one foot in front of the other; day after day and knowing that one day you will be back safely in your Master's arms. God's will, man does God's will.

2nd Chance: or is it really 77 Chances

"Then Peter approaching asked him, 'Lord, if my brother sins against me, how often must I forgive him? As many as seven times,' Jesus answered, 'I say to you, not seven times but seventy-seven times.'"[57]

Take a few moments and reflect on how many sins God has forgiven you over the course of your life, and imagine this number for a moment. Now, say thank you Father for forgiving me of these many sins! Both Barabbas and the second thief who died beside Christ were born as babies, just like Jesus was in Bethlehem. These men each had parents who I am sure loved them and cared for them for a part of their lives, certainly Jesus had a loving step-father and mother. Somewhere along these two men's journey they turned their eyes away from God and took a far different path than Jesus. Maybe they lost a parent while young, or a family member was killed, or maybe they grew up in a family that encouraged stealing, murder and lying. Whatever the reasons behind their sinful way of life they both were caught by the authorities and tried for their crimes and both were sentenced to die on the cross.

The second thief certainly fell into or chose the life he lived, he admitted to Christ that his crimes were worthy of his being put to death on the cross. The second thief recognized that there was a difference between what was right from wrong, and the second thief saw that Jesus was truly innocent of any sin and that Jesus didn't deserve to die on the cross. The second thief is important for us to remember, for we don't really know the time and day of our death, but as long as we are alive and breathing we can be forgiven from our sins. Jesus will know the state of your heart and judge whether you truly have given a heartfelt confession and he too will open the door to Paradise. We must develop a sense of urgency in turning our lives to Jesus, for

---

[57]   *Matt.18:21-22,NAB*

there will come a time when you will no longer be able to ask the Lord for forgiveness. Every day we hear of stories where people are killed in car accidents, or die from heart attacks, so don't waste a moment, stop and give your life to Jesus this moment, and take that first step onto that narrow path, it will be your most important step in your life.

The number seventy-seven so much doesn't represent the maximum number of times we can be forgiven, but it actually means that we are forgiven over and over until our very last breath on earth. God is not saying however that we can continue sinning every day without end; the forgiveness is there to help break us free from those sinful ways in which we live out our lives. When we sin, we are not doing the will of our Father in heaven. Whether we know it or not, our sins do have an impact in the world, a hurtful comment can ruin a marriage, or it can break a child's heart and spirit, often shaping how that person lives out their lives each day for years or even decades.

Does God know how our sins impact the world and the people in our lives? If we opened our eyes to God, we too would see the impact of our sins in our world. It is thought that Barabbas had killed someone, amongst his many crimes. What was the impact on that person's family? In most cases murder of a loved one is devastating on the family, and the effects of that loss may last a lifetime for some of the family members to be freed of that pain. Do you know that there are still people upset over the North winning the Civil War here in America? My own ancestors landed on Long Island with the hope of beginning a new life, serving and loving their God, but still they and the other settlers were in effect stealing the land the Native American Indians were living on at the time. Was it God's destiny that America was formed this way? I guess it depends upon your perspective, if you are a Native American it was seen as a great crime or sin, but if you were a white American you might think it was in our destiny that America was formed this way. My point being is that most of what we do can be understood by some as being sinful, while others might say it just is a part of our nature and not sinful at all. What does matter is whether God views the many areas of our life as being sinful or not.

In getting back to scripture where Peter is asking Jesus how many times are we to forgive those people in our life that have sinned against us, Jesus says not seven times, but seventy-seven times we are asked to forgive. Jesus is saying that we should show our forgiveness to others in much the same way that he has shown us his forgiveness when we have sinned against him, with total forgiveness and unconditional love. I know also that this isn't always the case with people, we may say we have forgiven someone on one level, but we hold back some of this forgiveness as a way to keep that person in check, or as a way to fill superior to them. And when we don't forgive a person totally we are in effect holding them hostage to our own will, preventing them from growing in their own faith, and maybe even turning them spiritually in a totally different direction in their life, perhaps even away from God.

CHAPTER 6

MERCY FROM ON HIGH

"The virtue of mercy is so beautiful and so highly esteemed by men that scarcely any other virtue is more highly praised, even those who have little consideration for God have practiced the works of mercy as a means of winning the praise and fame among men."[58]

How many times were we comforted as a child by our parents when we fell down and hurt our knee or scratched our palms? I have experienced mercy in my life on many occasions, it can be safe to say that everyone at one time in their life has been on the receiving end of mercy, and perhaps we have been the one showing mercy to another person. One of my most vivid memories I had as a child was when I slipped from the ladder going up into the hay mow, falling maybe fifteen feet and breaking my upper arm. I remember my brother walking me up to the house and having me lie down on the couch. I received a great deal of mercy and compassion from my whole family, the doctors and nurses during the day of the accident and on through my recovery time. Another example of mercy that was shown me was when as a young man I was facing an active phase of my neuromuscular disease and I was growing weaker, my parents took me back into their home and provided for my needs once again, most acts of mercy are born out of love for the person.

I remember a story my father once told us kids about an incident in a battle he was involved in during World War II,

---

[58] *p.185, excerpt used from "Summa of the Christian Life," Vol. 2, Tan Books, Charlotte, NC, used with permission, (www.tanbooks.com)*

during the Battle of the Bulge, his squad was under heavy fire and they were ordered to move forward towards a tree line, dad and one of his buddies were pinned down in a bomb crater and as they jumped out of the crater his friend was hit in the head with a bullet and fell back into the crater and into a pool of cold icy water. Dad turned around and went back to his friend because he couldn't stand to see his friend lying in the cold water, he went back in and pulled him out of the water and placed him along the rim of the crater, in lifting his body and holding up his head he had stuck his hand into his friend's brain. This was an act of mercy for a fellow brother in arms; this is one of many acts of mercy my dad showed others throughout his lifetime.

My Grandmother Linke was a young mother living in the heart of Berlin during World War II; she also had shown mercy to others on many occasions, one that sticks out was her willingness to stand in line for some Jewish ladies for some food. Doing this for a Jewish woman, put her on a list for the Gestapo, where the police would come and look for her on occasion in order to arrest her, but some local friends would tip her off and Grandma wouldn't go home for awhile, again an act of mercy on each of their parts.

As a nurse my mother loved working in a nursing home, everybody loved her because of her many acts of mercy she had shown them each day. Each one of my siblings and their spouses have demonstrated mercy over the course of their lives, as a parent in raising their children, in rescuing animals, as a nurse, as a special educator, as a foster parent, as a daughter helping a dying mother, as a soldier, as a business owner. Mercy is a part of all our lives; it guides our actions through life because it is an action that flows from God through us into the world.

Most every family, in every generation, all across the world have seen many of these same kinds of stories of mercy within their own family. I also know that there are some people who have rarely seen or experienced mercy within their lives. Look at Haiti, one of the poorest nations in the world; money, food, and supplies came in from many countries of the world after every hurricane or earthquake that struck this nation, all acts of mercy being shown to the people of these nations. I am a big fan of Maryknoll Brothers and Sisters—and their missions to the poorer countries of the world, a common story the priests or sister's often share about their work in these countries, is how generous these desperately poor people are to others, like sharing the last bits of food with you at a lunch that they had planned for you. Every week seems like a new tragedy for some country, from earthquakes, to hurricanes, to volcanoes, to floods, to fire, to tornadoes, to war, to crime and with all these tragedies comes millions and millions of acts of grace and mercy.

If we all take a moment now and reflect on these hundreds of billions of acts of mercy, we will realize that our lives and world are being flooded with constant acts of mercy, perhaps more now than ever before in history. God is calling us to be attentive in our lives and to be prepared for both in the giving and receiving of His mercy.

God's Mercy

"Then the eyes of both of them were opened, and they realized that they were naked; so they sewed fig leaves together and made loincloths for themselves. When they heard the sound of the Lord God moving about in the garden at the breezy time of the day, the man and his wife hid themselves from the Lord God among the trees of the garden. The Lord God then called to the man and asked him, 'Where are you?' He answered, 'I heard you in the garden; but I was afraid, because I was naked, so I hid myself.' Then he asked, 'Who told you that you were naked? You have eaten, then, from the tree of which I had forbidden you to eat!' The man replied, 'the woman whom you put here with me, she

*gave me fruit from the tree, so I ate it.' The Lord God
then asked the woman, 'Why did you do such a thing?'
The woman answered, 'the serpent tricked me into it,
and so I ate it.'"[59]*

Every person living today is born with this original sin and
we each have become separated from God in some manner
within each of our lives. It is God who always provides His
people with mercy, for God is mercy; His love for us is so great
that He even placed His own son Jesus on the cross, so that by
his death on the cross every person ever born is given a chance
to be freed from sin within their own lives. Everything in this
world was given to us by God; He gave us water to drink, or
God provided the food for our belly, it was God who made
the first clothes for Adam and Eve, it is God who provided
caves for shelter, or the materials we needed to make our own
homes. God gave us other people so we can learn to share and
be dependent upon each other. The Old Testament is filled with
story after story of God's love for His people, sharing His mercy
with the people of the world year after year, like Abraham,
Noah, Moses, David, the various Prophets, and through the
Jewish people.

Noah and his family lived during a time great violence and
wickedness, and God said *"I will wipe out from the earth the
men whom I created,"[60]* because of this great evil, but Noah
found favor with God because he was a righteous man, totally
blameless in his generation and he walked with God each day.
Noah listened to God and he did as God commanded, despite
the great effort in building this great Ark. He collected food for
the future, he collected pairs of every kind of animal and he
placed his family in the ark. Scripture says that the Lord sealed
them in the Ark. It was God's mercy who cleansed the earth of
evil, leaving Noah's righteous family to rebuild a world. The

---

[59]   *Gen.3:7-13,NAB*

[60]   *Gen.6:7,NAB*

world was given another chance to turn from sin and live a righteous life walking with God each day.

"The Lord said to Abram: 'go forth from the land of your kinsfolk and from your father's house to the land that I will show you. I will make you a great nation, and I will bless you, and make your name great, so that you will be a blessing, I will bless those who bless you, and curse those who curse you I will curse. All the communities of the earth shall find blessing in you.'" [61]

Abraham did as God commanded and moved his family towards Egypt. Abraham was a man of prayer, for he listened and heard what God wanted of him. Yet, he still was just a man, he still had doubts about his future—questioning God about having a son through his aged wife Sarah, or he didn't trust enough in God's mercy as he moved his family to Egypt, thus he gave his wife to the King so he could be safe. It was because of his distrust of God that God told Abraham that his descendents will become slaves in Egypt. But God corrected this mistake and brought the two back together, from then on he listened more closely to what the Lord wanted for his life: in where to live, in how he fought battles, in how he treated those he fought, in sacrificing animals, in having each male circumcised as a sign of a new covenant with God. In time Abraham was confident enough to argue with God over saving his nephew Lot in Sodom. Abraham's relationship with God continued to deepen with time. Abraham loved God so much that he was willing to sacrifice his own son Isaac for the Lord, because that was what the Lord willed for Abraham to do.

"Moses then cut two stone tablets like the former, and early the next morning he went up Mount Sinai as the Lord had commanded him, taking along the two stone

[61]   *Gen.12:1-3,NAB*

*tablets. Having come down in a cloud, the Lord stood
with him there and proclaimed his name, 'Lord.' Thus
the Lord passed before him and cried out, 'The Lord, the
Lord, a merciful and gracious God, slow to anger and
rich in kindness and fidelity, continuing his kindness
for a thousand generations, and forgiving wickedness
and crime and sin; yet not declaring the guilty guiltless,
but punishing children and grandchildren to the third
and fourth generation for their fathers' wickedness!'*[62]

Man's whole history is a story of our struggle living in a
world created by God, living with a God so present in our lives
that we can approach Him with our whole being, God sees us in
our all nakedness, meaning that there is nothing in our life that
is not known by God, especially our many sins. I have always
been encouraged by reading through the Old Testament for I
have seen many, many times where God has shown His mercy
to the people of the world. Even when He passed judgment on
an evil world, like with Noah, or the people of Sodom. God
wants our attention; He wants us to know him as much as He
knows us. Our God is not some distant God; He is a God who
wants to be a part of our lives. God's mercy is His constant
action and presence in our lives; it is a mercy that is there for
anyone to be changed by and made into a new person. Why
does God continue to share His mercy with you and me in this
great world of ours? It is because of His great love for us, He
fights for our future and the future of everyone alive; because
He wants us to return to Him in heaven. Our Father in heaven
knows that some of us will never make it back into heaven
because of our unwillingness to accept God's holy grace, but
God's love and grace still awaits your acceptance—even up to
your very last breath on earth.

62   *Ex.34:4-7,NAB*

Jesus' Mercy

"But early in the morning he arrived again in the temple area, and all the people started coming to him, and he sat down and taught them. Then the scribes and the Pharisees brought a woman who had been caught in adultery and made her stand in the middle. They said to him, 'Teacher, this woman was caught in the very act of committing adultery. Now in the law, Moses commanded us to stone such women. So what do you say?' They said this to test him, so that they could have some charge to bring against him. Jesus bent down and began to write on the ground with his finger. But when they continued asking him, he straightened up and said to them; 'Let the one among you who is without sin be the first to throw a stone at her.' Again he bent down and wrote on the ground. And in response, they went away one by one, beginning with the elders. So he was left alone with the woman before him. Then Jesus straightened up and said to her, 'Woman, where are they? Has no one condemned you?' She replied; 'No one, sir,' Then Jesus said, 'Neither do I condemn you. Go, (and) from now on do not sin anymore.' Jesus spoke to them again, saying, 'I am the light of the world. Whoever follows me will not walk in darkness, but will have the light of life.'"[63]

It is through our Lord Jesus that all mercy is given to the world, it is the reason he was given to the world, to be that Paschal Sacrifice for the sins of the world, for yours and my own sins. Every action in the Lord's life reflected God's love and mercy for the world. From his birth and up through the first thirty years of his life—loving and serving his family. Jesus' ministry years were filled with thousands of acts of

---

[63]   *John 8:2-12, NAB*

mercy leading up to his death on the cross at Calvary. And even following his death and resurrection the Lord's mercy still continues to flow through him into the world for all the ages, for all peoples across our whole world.

The sending of the angel Gabriel was in itself an act of mercy from God because it was time for the greatest act of mercy upon the world to begin. Our Father in heaven knew where a favored daughter was living, because Mary had lived her whole life serving God throughout her young life, God knew that her heart was pure and that she was always willing to serve Him in her life, so God sent Gabriel as a messenger to Mary, who informed her that she was chosen by God to bear the son of God. Mary gave her consent for this great act of mercy from God, allowing the Holy Spirit to do God's will and in time she bore a son named Jesus.

For you see that for every act of mercy requires at least two parties, the one who is willing to provide the act of mercy and the other who is willing to receive the act of mercy. Without the Virgin Mary's willingness to accept God's mercy, our world might not have been given God's son. Mary's purity and closeness with God allowed her to become that pure vessel which allowed God's only son to form within her womb. Jesus' birth has helped transform the world for all of history, for we now have a God who walks and breathes as a man, a God who knows us as a man living under the same constraints as any other person in the world.

The humbleness of being born in a stable inside a cave shows us how much our Father in heaven truly loves us, Jesus was not born into some fancy house fit for a king, but a lowly stable where cows and sheep came to eat their food and rest from the cold night. Every person born in this world is born totally dependent upon their parents for their very survival, Jesus was no different, he suckled at his mother's breast, he ate the food and drank the water and wine his parents provided for him each day, he lived under the roof of a home his parents provided for him, he learned the skills of his step-father's trade, his faith was formed by his parent's lives and how they gave their lives to God. Jesus lived this way for thirty years; he received many, many acts of mercy from his parents. I have always wondered about these hidden years for Jesus and his family. Why did the Lord wait until he was thirty years old to begin his ministry? Why not begin his ministry when he was eighteen; for he surely was considered a man by this age? His whole life reflected the will of his Father in heaven. At the age of thirty, the time for Jesus to begin his ministry was preordained by his Father in heaven, the world was now ready to hear God's message through the mouth of Jesus.

How was it that Jesus set out to change the world? Did he take off by himself and share his Father's message with the world alone? No, Jesus surrounded himself with people, his twelve chosen Apostles who would become the repository of this special message from God, and there were many others that followed Jesus from the beginning, all believing in the message brought to the world from their Lord. The message was first taught to those first followers of Jesus, but he also taught God's message to the everyday folks. With the occasional large crowds Jesus primarily taught by using simple parables taken from life, which most people could easily recognize and understand from their own experiences in life.

Have you ever bought a book whose message was written for a specific group of people outside your interest area, like quantum physics? I did, but in no time I lost interest in the material for I couldn't relate to anything being talked about in the book. I much prefer reading those books where the authors wrote at my own level of understanding, because the words within this book will have a greater potential for touching my heart. Jesus preferred sharing those common everyday stories that touched the lives of the people, but we must also recognize that Jesus still felt it important to instruct his Apostles with the full message and plan of his Father in heaven. Scripture also tells us that rarely his Apostles fully understood what Jesus was saying to them, but Jesus still shared this knowledge with them anyway, he knew that one day they would understand the totality of his message. It was only after the Lord's resurrection and the sending of the Holy Spirit did his Apostles begin to understand all of Christ's teachings. One example of a scripture: "*I have told you this in figures of speech. The hour is coming when I will no longer speak to you in figures but I will tell you clearly about the Father.*"[64]

I have read through the bible a number of times and each time the scripture opens up to me in different ways. I might have read the scripture a dozen times, but at this specific time this same scripture touched my heart in a special way, due in part to the work of the Holy Spirit. I also think that Jesus and the Holy Spirit opens our heart and minds to the message from the scripture at those specific moments in our lives, as a way that draws us closer to him in faith. So we can see that every act of mercy occurs at those moments when we are in need of some form of help, a mercy that encourages us in our own faith, a mercy that always draw our eyes to the giver and beyond.

These simple stories were gifts of mercy given to us from Jesus. Jesus also knew that he would die on the cross, so he surrounded himself with his Apostles and taught them about God, he knew that one day he would not be there in person to teach about God's love and mercy. So his Apostles would become the foundation on which his Church was formed, for it was through these men his message would be taken out into the world. After Pentecost, each of the Apostles was infused with the Holy Spirit, and with the Holy Spirit's direction the Apostles now fully understood what their Lord had taught them during those years of ministry.

Jesus came into a world that was broken, the people had lost the ability to truly change their own lives and give the full measure of their love to God. Jesus understood the suffering and isolation that people felt from their various disabilities or illnesses, so he cured the blind, he healed the deaf, he cured a

---

64   *John 16:25,NAB*

man of his violent seizures, he healed a man so he could walk again, and he also freed a man from his demons. Who can forget those stories where Jesus brought a child back to life, or his friend Lazarus coming back to life? Our Father in heaven sent Jesus into the world for two specific purposes, to teach the world about His truth and to allow Jesus to suffer and die on the cross for our sins. This great act of love and mercy forever changed the world for all of eternity. Even during Jesus' final moments on the cross we see Jesus showing mercy, in giving his mother to his friend John, and in promising a thief that by the end of the day he would see him in heaven.

"While they were eating, Jesus took bread, said the blessing, broke it, and giving it to his disciples said, 'Take and eat; this is my body.' Then he took a cup, gave thanks, and gave it to them, saying, 'Drink from it, all of you, for this is my blood of the covenant, which will be shed on behalf of many for the forgiveness of sins.'"[65]

Holy Spirit's Mercy as a Comforter

The Holy Spirit is often referred as the Comforter, a perfect sign of our Father's mercy and love for the world, another visible sign of God coming into our world, Jesus came that we may see and know God's presence as a man. The Holy Spirit was given so we might know and understand the truth and message of Jesus Christ within our life. Remember how the Holy Spirit transformed the Apostles at Pentecost, the Apostles finally understood all that Jesus had taught them through those three years, and these men were no longer afraid of proclaiming Lord Jesus to the world. The Holy Spirit was given to the world as another act of mercy, an act that will always be with us on earth unto the end of time.

---

[65] *Matt. 26:26-28, NAB*

Both of my parents died about thirty years ago and there isn't a day that goes by that I don't wish that my mom and dad were still alive and well and a vital part of my life. I loved them with all my heart; their presence in my life shaped every aspect of my life. I remember the pain of separation I felt when they were buried in the earth, forever gone physically from my life. In time I recognized that their love and all they had taught me will always be with me throughout my whole life, through the love they gave their family, friends, community and country. The Holy Spirit was given to us in the world as a reminder of how Jesus had shaped the world. It is the Holy Spirit that we use to pray to the Lord, it is the Holy Spirit who teaches us those truths that Jesus taught about God.

"If you love me, you will keep my commandments. And I will ask the Father, and he will give you another Advocate to be with you always, the Spirit of truth, which the world cannot accept, because it neither sees nor knows it. But you know it, because it remains with you, and will be in you. I will not leave you orphans; I will come to you."[66]

Holy Spirit's Mercy as an Advocate

When I was a child I sometimes needed to be disciplined by either my mother or father for some action that was wrong: cussing, having a smart mouth, fighting with my sister, or disobeying a task they asked of me. In order for any house to run smoothly, especially when nine people lived in a home, discipline was an important tool for keeping the household running smoother, siblings that got along, doing the chores that needed to be done each day, and showing respect to each other was very important to my parents. Our parents were our Advocates; they taught us about what was right and what was wrong.

---

[66]   *John 14:15-18,NAB*

Without the Holy Spirit's presence in the world, Jesus might have been forgotten to history, the first Apostles already struggled with their faith, especially with their leader gone from their midst. All of the Lord's teachings hadn't taken hold yet in their lives and with time they might have forgotten parts of his teachings. As an Advocate, the Holy Spirit has the potential for opening up each of our faiths to the greater truths that the Lord has for us and the world. We will each know those areas in our life that do not belong to God, we will know how to live out our lives with righteousness, a life lived in knowing Jesus so intimately that his breath becomes our breath and his arms become our arms, and his love becomes our love in all its purity. We can only know the Father through what Jesus tells us, and we can know Jesus by the many actions of the Holy Spirit and by the actions of the Church that Jesus formed through the first Apostles.

"But because I told you this, grief has filled your hearts. But I tell you the truth, it is better for you that I go. For if I do not go, the Advocate will not come to you. But if I go, I will send him to you. And when he comes he will convict the world in regard to sin and righteousness and condemnation: sin, because they do not believe in me; righteousness, because I am going to the Father and you will no longer see me; condemnation, because the ruler of this world has been condemned."[67]

Our Mercy

Our Lord gives us scriptures like those found in the Book of Tobit; that explain to us the importance of being merciful within our lives of faith. Our lives are not one where we can sit on our hands and do nothing and still expect God's grace. Our model is Jesus, his truth and life for us flows from his

---

[67]   *John 16:6-11,NAB*

father, everything Jesus did while in the world flowed from his Father's will. It is the same for you and I in this world, for we each play a part in this world, we each are given special gifts which the Lord needs for his use in the world. Pope John Paul II was a man who literally touched over two billion people's lives by being the man Jesus called him to be, an Apostle in his Church. Pope John Paul II shared his gifts of the Spirit with the world: through his wisdom of God's truth, through his ability to share his knowledge of Jesus, by the example in the way he lived out his faith, by the gifts of healing when he placed his hands on the people who needed healing, by being able to discern the spirits and their effect on a person's life, but his greatest gift was his capacity for loving everyone. Pope John Paul II's daily life was one of deep prayer and service to the people of God.

My sister Sandy and her husband Don, felt called by Jesus to open up their home to foster children: 1) to kids fleeing from Vietnam 2) to local children in the area. These boys and girls became a part of their family and they saw each of these children as being a gift from God. In a sense they become each child's advocate, giving each child a stable home, teaching them about their love for Jesus, surrounding them with love and protection.

My sister Sandy was expecting their second child, but Emily decided to be born early, weighing a little over a pound and about the size of Don's hand. Both Don and Sandy surrounded their little girl with love, showering her with kisses and prayers, they held this beautiful child for three hours before she breathed her last breath. Her desire for life truly touched their lives forever and they were blessed by her presence in the world, her life had value and was important to God, she fulfilled her part in God's plan.

Kelly was one of my students, she had such a fiery spirit, she never was able to talk, but you sure knew what she was thinking, she had a great sense of humor, she loved playing tricks on you, and she would laugh and laugh. She had a number of medical problems that impacted every aspect of her life, she died at a real young age, but her life was filled with the love from her family, and the love of friends and teachers. Her love for life and fiery spirit touched each of our lives, and I know I was blessed to have known her in my life, her life taught me so much about Jesus and how we are to entrust our lives and future with Him.

"But as it is, God placed the parts, each one of them, in the body as he intended. If they were all one part, where would the body be? But as it is, there are many parts, yet one body. The eye cannot say to the hand, I do not need you, nor again the head to the feet, I do not need you. Indeed, the parts of the body that seem to be weaker are all the more necessary, and those parts of the body that we consider less honorable we surround with greater honor, and our less presentable parts are treated with greater propriety, whereas our more presentable parts do not need this. But God has so constructed the body as to give greater honor to a part that is without it, so that there may be no division in the body, but that the parts may have the same concern for one another. If (one) part suffers, all the parts suffer with it; if one part is honored, all the parts share its joy." [68]

Where do we fit into this Body of Christ? It depends upon which physical and spiritual gifts you were given at birth, gifts that can either be enriched or hindered by the way we have chosen to live out our lives, or by what we have learned from our families and neighborhoods, or what we have learned from the greater society, but especially by what we have learned from Jesus. Only Jesus knows us better than we know ourselves, only he knows where we are in his body. Pope John Paul II had his role in the world, as did Emily, as does my sister Sandy and her

---

[68]   *1 Cor.12:18-26,NAB*

husband Don, as did my student Kelly. We each are called to be in this world for a specific purpose and that is to do the will of our Lord Jesus, if it is to be an Apostle, or if we are called to be a parent, or whether we are called to be a child struggling with major health problems, then this is what God wants for our lives. My friend John always knew that he wanted to become a farmer and he became one after high school.

Even the loss of hundreds of millions of babies who have died as a result of abortion is not wasted, for their loss is a stark reminder about the selfishness and evil actions of a nation. The loss of so many babies mean that we each need to become more prayerful as a part of this Body of Christ and we need to open our hearts and minds in healing this broken part of the body, we need to show mercy and love to the parents of these precious babies. Can we ever imagine the loss of all those spiritual and intellectual gifts that could have been used to transform the world and make it a better place to live? Nothing is wasted, evil is allowed, natural and manmade disasters, wars, famine, everything has value and purpose, if it turns people's eyes towards the Lord.

When we face the extent of our sins within our lives through the grace and mercy flowing from the cross, and we allow the Holy Spirit to bring our darkness out into the light, we can finally see our sins impact on our life and those people around us in the world. Jesus died on the cross, so the impact of these sins would no longer be a part of our lives and we can truly be born again into a new life. Jesus death was the greatest act of love and mercy in the history of the world; nothing will ever come close to this one act of love. It becomes our choice whether to accept this great gift or we can let it slip from our hands and do nothing.

We are not alone in this world, we are just one person out of over seven billion people and every person is loved and valued by God. How we treat each other is important to God! And we do this by showing love and mercy to everyone within our world. No longer can we think that we are better than the other parts of the body, for we all belong to Christ's body. Christ just didn't die for the Christians, he died for the Muslims, he died for the Jewish people, he died for the Hindu people, he died for all those who call themselves atheists, he died for us all because it was the will of his Father in heaven. But, how can this be? It is not our place to judge in who is and who is not going to heaven. Did God assign you the task of being the Judge over who is and who isn't going to heaven? Scripture tells us that Jesus was given this great and holy task by God.

"Do you see that the good of this life and those of the life to come are promised to the merciful? Hence, if your heart is not moved to the practice of this virtue by reason of the promise of spiritual goods, here you have what you desire, namely temporal goods. Heed the words of the Savior when he says, 'Give, and it shall be given to you.'"[69]

---

[69] *p. 200, excerpt used from "Summa of the Christian Life," Vol. 2, Tan Books, Charlotte, NC, used with permission, (www.tanbooks.com)*

CHAPTER 7

PATH TO GOD: TOUCHING HEAVEN

"In the beginning, when God created the heavens and the earth, the earth was a formless wasteland, and darkness covered the abyss, while a mighty wind swept over the waters. Then God said, 'Let there be light,' and there was light. God saw how good the light was. God then separated the light from the darkness. God called the light 'day,' and the darkness he called 'night.' Thus evening came, and morning followed, the first day."

"Then God said, 'Let there be a dome in the middle of the waters, to separate one body of water from the other.' And so it happened: God made the dome, and it separated the water above the dome from the water below it. God called the dome 'the sky.' Evening came, and morning followed, the second day."

"Then God said, 'Let the water under the sky be gathered into a single basin, so that the dry land may appear.' And so it happened: the water under the sky was gathered into its basin, and the dry land appeared. God called the dry land 'the earth and the basin of the water he called the sea.' God saw how good it was. Then God said, 'Let the earth bring forth vegetation: every kind of plant that bears seed and every kind of fruit tree on earth that bears fruit with its seed in it.' And so it happened: the earth brought forth every kind of plant that bears seed and every kind of fruit tree on earth that bears fruit with its seed in it. God saw how good it was. Evening came, and morning followed, the third day."

"Then God said: 'Let there be lights in the dome of the sky, to separate day from night. Let them mark the fixed times, the days and the years, and serve as luminaries in the dome of the sky, to shed light upon the earth.' And so it happened: God made the two great lights, the greater one to govern the day, and the lesser one to govern the night; and he made the stars. God set them in the dome of the sky, to shed light upon the earth, to govern the day and the night, and to separate the light from the darkness. God saw how good it was. Evening came, and morning followed, the fourth day."

"Then God said, 'Let the water teem with an abundance of living creatures, and on the earth let birds fly beneath the dome of the sky.' And so it happened: God created the great sea monsters and all kinds of swimming creatures with which the water teems, and all kinds of winged birds. God saw how good it was, and God blessed them, saying, 'Be fertile, multiply, and fill the water of the seas; and let the birds multiply on the earth.' Evening came, and morning followed, the fifth day."

"Then God said, 'Let the earth bring forth all kinds of living creatures: cattle, creeping things, and wild animals of all kinds.' And so it happened: God made all kinds of wild animals, all kinds of cattle, and all kinds of creeping things of the earth. God saw how good it was. Then God said: 'Let us make man in our image, after our likeness. Let them have dominion over the fish of the sea, the birds of the air, and the cattle, and over all the wild animals and all the creatures that crawl on the ground.' God created man in his image; in the divine image He created him; male and female he created them. God blessed them, saying: 'Be fertile and multiply; fill the earth and subdue it. Have dominion over the fish of the sea, the birds of the air, and all the

*living things that move on the earth.' God also said:
'See, I give you every seed-bearing plant all over the
earth and every tree that has seed-bearing fruit on it to
be your food; and to all the animals of the land, all the
birds of the air, and all the living creatures that crawl
on the ground, I give all the green plants for food.' And
so it happened. God looked at everything he had made,
and he found it very good. Evening came, and morning
followed, the sixth day."*

*"Thus the heavens and the earth and all their array
were completed. Since on the seventh day God was
finished with the work he had been doing, he rested on
the seventh day from all the work he had undertaken.
So God blessed the seventh day and made it holy,
because on it he rested from all the work he had done
in creation."*[70]

Why am I placing these scriptures from Genesis back
into the book a second time? I believe we each need to be
reminded once again as to who created the world, and who is
responsible for virtually every atom and substance in this world
and universe.

It is obvious if we read the newspaper or watch any news
program today we see a world that is careening out of control
and on the brink of a collapse. We are living in a world that has
forgotten who God is to the world. We are living in a world that
is losing its own consciousness for what is a sin or not. Our world
is filled with folks who have eaten from the tree of knowledge
and decided that they are capable of making decisions that are
both right and wrong for their lives, even better than what God
would want for them. But, God is telling us so clearly in every
scripture that we will never be God, because we will never have
that kind of power to judge correctly. So, how can God break

---

[70]   *Gen.1:1-32 and Gen.2:1-3,NAB*

this cycle of sin that now threatens all life on earth? God the Father does it through His son Jesus Christ.

Our Father in heaven is our Creator, He created our world and He created each of us. Mankind has built some very remarkable buildings that reach for the heavens, but they are made from the materials that God made in the first place. Our food, our drink, our clothes, the homes we live in, or the cars we drive, our toys, even the air we breathe is all created by God. If we want to eat, then we have to plant the seeds that God has provided for us into the ground, we as God's children must participate and subdue the world we live in, meaning our survival is dependent upon the efforts we make to put food and drink on our table. It is God's light and rain which allows our food to grow in the dirt He provided for the seeds. God speaks, the world responds. God speaks, we respond!

Touching heaven is what prayer does for us each day; it is the closest activity most of us will ever have in reliving our time in the Garden of Eden. The scriptures from Genesis explain that it is because of God that our world and our very existence are possible. Adam and Eve's sin in the Garden becomes our own sin in that when we sin we become more distant from our God in heaven; we have lost that close and open relationship we once had with God.

For a day, Adam worked alongside God and put a name to every animal, creature and thing in our world. Even today we hear of discoveries of new species, either alive or found in ancient fossils, never before seen by today's world, and so we give those new species a name of our choosing. Every parent ponders over the naming of their children, or for the pets they own. The naming of something created by God is important because it unites us as a person to this child, or this pet, or this object in a powerful way; it forms our life and changes our future in so many different ways. As Adam and Eve lived within the Garden they were united with God in a unique way, unashamed before their God, loving God because He was their God. Heaven and earth were united together because God formed it that way, but when Adam and Eve sinned, they were banned from the Garden of Eden and were then forced to live in the earthly world. Adam and Eve's lives were forever changed because of their sin, much in the same way our own sins change our own closeness with God, and so we are forever striving between the hardness of our lives and the sublimity of God. My favorite memories in my life are when I have come into contact with God or Jesus in some powerful way, and in finding God in the day in and day out of the cycle of life. I will share one memory right now. Back in 1989, while on a retreat on a beach in Maine I experienced God in such a way where I never doubted God again about His presence in the world. It was a five day retreat where we focused on various topics, attended daily Mass, and we spent lots of time in prayer. Each morning I got up around 2:00 am and walked out onto the beach with a chair and just sat by the ocean watching, listening to the surf washing in and out for those early morning hours, observing the sun rise in those early hours was truly breathtaking. Oh, yes I prayed prayers of thanksgiving, but mostly I listened for the Lord's voice within my heart, on the third morning God filled my heart in such a way that I knew God loved His world so very much.

The Apostles Creed begins with "I believe in God the Father," I really "do" believe God is our Father and that this world we live in, is really His world. It never really was our world in the first place; even though at times we think we are in control of our little part of the world. Like Adam and Eve we might think we can be like God and eat that apple, that we can control every aspect of our lives—maybe in some sense we do by our choices in life, but we don't have the power over life and death, we may have the power to take a life of another, or our own life, but we don't have any power over the essence of the Spirit that God breathed into our body. Our sinful actions may subdue the Spirit's role in our life, but it will be God through Jesus who will decide our fate upon our death, on Judgment Day.

In reading scripture about when Moses went up Mt. Sinai to meet God, I realized that God in turn also made the effort and came down from heaven to meet with Moses. It reminded me of how far apart we as humans are from our God in heaven. One of my favorite priests Father Al Lauer explained that if every person who called themselves a Christian, actually lived as Christ calls us to live, the world would be a far different place than what we have today. So, he is telling us that there is something within us that separates us from others, but it also separates us from God as well. And like Adam and Eve it is our sins that will keep us isolated from our God and isolated from other people.

In reading Uncle Tom's Cabin by Harriet Beecher Stowe, a book that changed a nation, within the book is a dialogue that describes the many different people in how they either believed or was against the institution of slavery. Many of these individuals professed to be Christians, while others stated they didn't recognize God at all. Some folks loved and respected the work these slaves did for them, but these slaves were still viewed as property to be bought and sold as needed. There were several families that took in escaped slaves and helped them to begin a new life. One man inherited a number of slaves from his father, he was attached to them, but he was against the idea of slavery, but yet he didn't want to sell them or give them their freedom either, because he feared for their lives and for their future if left alone against the world they lived in at that time. His brother primarily used hundreds of slaves as a way to increase his wealth on the plantation. This brother also didn't have a problem in disciplining his slaves, to get them to work correctly.

The one brother had an elderly woman cousin come down from Vermont and stay with them, so she could watch over his sick daughter. This cousin was dead set against the idea of slavery, but she didn't quite understand why her nephew would not give up his slaves, even though he was against the idea of slavery as well. Augustine gave his cousin a nine year old girl to do with as she wishes, and this woman struggled in trying to teach this girl the proper way to live, she even used her hand against her—to get her to subdue her spirit. She was taken aback that even she was willing to raise her hand against another person. I guess my point in sharing these thoughts on slavery is that life can be very complicated, what is right and what is wrong can be hard for us to see at different times in our lives.[71]

A different Augustine's whole youth was spent in following the things of the world, steeped in various levels of sin as told by him in a book he wrote. There came a time within his life where God broke through that fog of sin and changed his path in life. Today, we see St. Augustine as a Doctor of the Catholic Church and whose teachings and writings have brought millions of people back to Christ.

What inside me has kept me from experiencing God in a more real way? Was I blind or deaf like some of those folks in scripture? Do we seek out our God, or does he seek us out in our busy lives? For me at least, I have a strong desire to be working at some type of a job, working on the family history, or reading daily news and reading books for deepening my faith—making notes that I might use in future books I am called to write. I always have some type of music/tv/noise going—in many ways to keep me company, but it also affects my ability for listening to Jesus each day. With my personality, I have always found it easier to experience God's presence in the world by being out in nature, like sitting by the ocean, or sitting on a mountaintop, or the edge of the Grand Canyon, or by sitting by a lake, or deep in the woods, and best of all by sitting before the tabernacle.

In re-reading this scripture on Mt. Sinai and Moses a proverbial "light bulb" turned on in my mind that I could still go to these places everyday from the comfort of my home, by using

---

[71] *p.222, "Uncle Tom's Cabin," Harriet Beecher Stowe, Dover Publications, Inc., Mineola, NY, originally written in 1852, republished 2005, (paraphrased from book, no actual quotes used)*

webcams. I spend time in prayer every day before the Eucharist at a church in Louisville, I watch a sunrise over a beach in South Carolina, or sit on a mountain top in the Smoky Mountains, or I observe the Great Niagara Falls in Canada. My world is not so small now, and it gives me an opportunity for praying for those people in those areas, so God uses anything to keep our eyes focused on the pathway, so we can see where Jesus is leading us.

As a young child I had the ability to run and walk up or down a mountain side, so I have some sense as to the amount of energy and effort it would take to go up a mountain, albeit a small one. I have always marveled at a person's ability for climbing up the face of mountains, grasping the smallest of foot ledges as they worked their way higher to the top of the mountain. We know why Moses climbed Mt. Sinai to meet God, but why are there some people today who risk their lives in climbing mountains all over the world? Are they climbing to the top to meet God? Or is there another reason? I do know one thing that God will make Himself known to that person over and over on the trip going up or down that mountain. Each person will have gained some insight into the strength of their character, and they will be given a chance to be marveled by the grandeur of not our world, but God's world.

How many of us know when a sparrow has fallen to the ground? Our God sees all and knows about everything that is going on this world, in every nation, in every state, in every county, in every town, on every street corner, in every home, in every room. If God knows when a bird falls to the ground, doesn't that tell us how much God cares for all of His creatures? These scriptures also point out how much more important we are as humans to God, for we were given something that animals or any other creature never was given, God breathed into us and gave us our soul. How else do you think God knows everything about us, a part of God resides within our body, God even knows the number of hairs on our head. No one in our lives, neither our spouse, nor our parents, nor our friends and church pastors know us in the same way God knows you right now, in this very moment—both the good and the bad parts of our life.

God walked with us in the Garden of Eden, He knew Adam and Eve so intimately, the very same way He knows each of us today, you see, God never did take His eyes off of us, even when we are sinning, not once, not ever. It is we who have turned our eyes away from God, to eat the forbidden fruit in the garden, not God, but you and me. The books of the Old Testament remind us that the people of the world have always fought this great battle over the future of our soul, a battle between which path we will choose to follow in the world, between good and evil, between the Lord's path and the wide road of the world, one path leads to heaven and one road leads to hell.

It was mankind who turned their eyes from God and followed their own path in the world, but it is God that still continues to come down from heaven and intervenes in our world; we've seen it happen in Egypt, we have seen it happen on Mt. Sinai, we have seen it happen with Abraham and Sarah, we have seen it happen with King David, we have seen it happen through the many Prophets of Israel, and we have seen it happen with the birth of God's son in Bethlehem. Our God, our Father loves each of us beyond all measure, no matter what we have done in our world, God is always ready to celebrate our return to Him.

It is time for us to climb Mt. Sinai where we can come before God the Father and finally accept His great love for us. The ball is in our court, we must now take on our responsibility and make that effort and seek God out on that mountain, we must search for that burning bush on this great mountain and we must approach this bush knowing that God has made it holy because He is holy. We must gather our gold, frankincense, and myrrh (our special gifts given to us by God) and follow the star of Bethlehem and search for Jesus in the world, and when we find him in the stable we will know he is a King worthy of us to follow the rest of our lives, and we will give to Jesus all that we are as a man or woman of the world.

CHAPTER 8

PATH TO GOD: A MESSAGE FROM THE CROSS

"Jesus cried out in a loud voice, 'Father, into your hands I commend my spirit;' and when he had said this he breathed his last."[72]

This one statement from Jesus sums up the culmination of Jesus' whole life. Every breath, every thought, every word, every prayer, every action was in doing the Father's will in God's world. Jesus from his very birth was dependent upon his parents. Jesus accepted the food, drink, clothes and the home his parents had provided. Jesus learned the trade as a carpenter from his step-father Joseph, which for a time helped support his mother following the death of Joseph. Scripture gives us only glimpses of the kind of man Jesus would become in his life, his knowledge and understanding of scripture marveled some of the priests at the Great Temple in Jerusalem, and we know that Jesus was always obedient to his parents. But we finally get to see Jesus through the eyes and memories of his Apostles, sharing the journey they once shared with Jesus, and still continue to share with the world today through the words of the Holy Scripture and the oral teachings of the Catholic Church.

Jesus birth had been foretold for a thousand years, so why was the time that Jesus was born so important, a moment so momentous that the Church changed the calendar to begin a new century at 0 AD. God was preparing the world for His son Jesus, born at a time where prophecy after prophecy was

---

[72] *Luke 23:46, NAB*

being fulfilled, in preparing the minds and hearts of the people in Israel—especially those folks involved in this great act of history: Kings, Priests, scribes, Virgin Mary, Joseph, Mary's cousin Elizabeth, the child John the Baptist growing inside Elizabeth, the twelve men who will be asked one day by Jesus to drop their nets and follow him at a moment's notice, and the thousands of other people involved in this one of-a-kind world event.

I also want to make it clear that God is not this Grand Puppeteer who controls each of our lives as if we didn't matter, we do matter to Him; God loves us beyond all measure. If God was in complete control of our lives, our world would be devoid of all sin and evil, but as you can see, sin is everywhere you look. Our God doesn't say I think this person needs to be killed today, or that person raped, or that person should be robbed, or that man over there should have an affair with another man's wife, nor would he tell that veteran to live under the Rt.#105 expressway. Each of us is given free will, which means we have the right to choose the direction we take in life, and that being the right to follow the Lord on the narrow path, or the right in choosing to sin against our God.

A woman or a man that was raped didn't have a choice in this senseless act of evil; nor did that family ask to be robbed of their valued possessions, but these terrible actions are the consequence and nature of sin, not necessarily our own sins, but the sins of others that were directed towards these victims. All sins from great to small bring harm to God's world; some sins like murder or rape bring greater harm to the world.

During a small group prayer time while on retreat God granted me an experience for understanding the level of the pain and anguish He has for just one small country, the people of Nicaragua, this glimpse from the Lord maybe lasted for just a second or two, but the pain of this glimpse seared my heart, to this day I still pray for the people of this nation. This one second was more than I could bear, I can't even begin to imagine the pain and anguish God feels for the whole world He created.

I believe I was given this gift because it propels me forward with Christ, it encourages me to work all that much harder in those tasks that Jesus needs done through me each day. I can't take away this burden from God, but I can love and honor Him more each day by living through Jesus and following his will. My sister Sandy and I have built up a family tree going back several thousand years, and if I tried to figure out how many grandparents we had just for our family, it would be a number with maybe one hundred numbers long, a huge number of grandparents, certainly way more than all the people every born on the earth. I have had many grandparents over the years that have moved from Europe to America, marrying others from other parts of the country. My own father was born in Illinois, but he met and fell in love with a woman from Berlin, whom he met following the end of World War II. My wife was born in S. Korea, and she mostly grew up in Pakistan, and yet God brought the two of us together in marriage here in Illinois. My point is that only God has the vision and ability to transcend time and place and shape both the nations and the world by bringing people together and for raising up the world's leaders and teachers, men like St. Francis who brought most of Europe back to God, or the Cure of Ars in France, or Mother Theresa of Calcutta, India, and Pope John Paul II, and many others as well.

As one human being living among seven billion other people, we each can only see just one tiny part of the overall world, while God knows each man, woman and child by name, He deeply knows each of our hearts, and only God can see the big picture because God is the Creator of all life. Think of us as one large seven billion piece puzzle, each of us are closely connected to those people in our area of the puzzle, but only God can observe the totality of his world puzzle, only God has ties to each person of the world. His breath, His Spirit resides within each person, in people of all colors, in people of every faith, in people of no faith, and in people from every country and nation. Our pathway back to heaven is now possible because

God our Father provided us the way, a pathway through His son Jesus.

In the last chapter we explored the lengths from which our Father in heaven has continually explored ways to give people a way to find their way back to that closeness with God that we once had in heaven:

1. Cleansing the world of evil through the great flood
2. Calling Abraham to move his family to the Promised land
3. Freeing a nation from slavery in Egypt
4. Freedom from death through the Passover
5. As a way to live—Ten Commandments
6. Calling up a shepherd, named David, to become a King of Israel, a King who transformed a nation
7. Building a Great Temple where God can be worshipped, building the Tabernacle from where the tablets were placed
8. Allowing the Israel nation to be conquered and dispersed throughout the area and destroying the Great Temple
9. Calling out Prophets to help bring people back to God and to Israel

Can we begin to see how much our God truly loves us yet? Why does God care about our future? Why does He keep trying to change the direction of our lives? Does God need us for some purpose? What does God see within us that has value to Him? We know that God is concerned with all things, He knows when a sparrow falls to the ground, and He certainly knows all of our pains and hurts because we are of greater value to Him, because of the soul that He had placed within our bodies. Our value to God is that we fully belong to God, a part of God resides within our bodies, and He loves us as a Father loves His children. Scripture tells us that through Jesus we become the adopted sons and daughters of God.

"But scripture confined all things under the power of sin that through faith in Jesus Christ the promise might be given to those who believe. Before faith came, we were held in custody under law, confined for the faith that was to be revealed. Consequently, the law was our disciplinarian for Christ, that we might be justified by faith. But now that faith has come, we are no longer under a disciplinarian. For through faith you are all children of God in Christ Jesus. For all of you who were baptized into Christ have clothed yourselves with Christ. There is neither Jew nor Greek, there is neither slave nor free person, there is not male and female; for you are all one in Christ Jesus. And if you belong to Christ, then you are Abraham's descendant, heirs according to the promise."[73]

Last night I was drawn to watch an old movie about Helen Keller and Anne Sullivan. Helen was a young girl, totally blind, mostly deaf and totally out of control from her parent's point of view. Anne Sullivan was a young woman who was slowly going blind from a childhood disease, but Anne had studied to become a teacher of the blind and deaf. Helen's parents didn't place much hope for their daughter's future, they only wanted Helen to act like a lady, and learn a certain level of independence and decorum.

Anne saw a different kind of future for Helen, a world of learning and using knowledge for the good of mankind. Anne taught Helen those skills that increased her independence, eating, drinking, manners, acting appropriately, but more importantly Anne wanted to open Helen's world to knowledge. Helen struggled in connecting the letters of the words to the objects that Anne was signing into her hand, in the final scene of the movie, the family wanted to celebrate Helen's gains with a family meal.

---

[73] *Gal.3:22-29,NAB*

During the meal Helen kept throwing down her napkin, Anne picked it up once, and the mother picked it up a second time. Anne wanted Helen to be responsible for her own action, so she pulled her away from the table, and Helen threw the water pitcher filled with water all over Anne. A big battle erupts with parents passing excuses over their daughter's behavior; Anne strongly felt that Helen needed to accept the responsibility for her own life. Anne drags Helen out to the water pump with the water pitcher as the catalyst; Helen needed to fill the pitcher with water. It was at this moment when Helen's "light bulb" turned on and that she finally understood that the letters that was now being spelled into her hand was what was now running through her fingers, namely water.[74]

Her life and world was now forever changed because she now had the understanding that those word spellings actual meant a specific thing, person or action in her world. Everything our God has ever done for the world since man's fall from the Garden of Eden is directed to opening our minds and Spirit to the depth of His love for us, God is constantly spelling the word Jesus into our palm each day; with the hope that one day we may recognize the kind of love that God has for us this day. Do we remain blind and deaf to what God is spelling into our hand, or do we finally understand what this love means for our life? Does this new knowledge of God's love heal the brokenness within our lives and give us the courage and strength to expand our world, both in changing the direction of our life and in the way we are called to live each day, by accepting God's love through Jesus?

Jesus was given to the world, so we as sons and daughters of the first earthly Adam and Eve and who are still attached to the way of life that takes us away from God, for it will be the

---

[74]   *The Miracle Worker, 1967, William Gibson, based on autobiography of Helen Keller, "The Story of my Life," published, 1902 (paraphrased from movie, did not use any actual quotes)*

grace we received from Jesus that will give us an opportunity for changing the direction we are going in life.

"In many and various ways God spoke of old to our fathers by the prophets, but in these last days he has spoken to us by a Son." Christ, the Son of God made man, is the Father's one, perfect and unsurpassable Word. In him he has said everything; there will be no other word than this one. St. John of the Cross, among others, commented strikingly on Hebrews 1:1-2: In giving us his Son, his only Word (for he possesses no other), he spoke everything to us at once in this sole Word - and he has no more to say. . . because what he spoke before to the prophets in parts, he has now spoken all at once by giving us the All Who is His Son. Any person questioning God or desiring some vision or revelation would be guilty not only of foolish behaviour but also of offending him, by not fixing his eyes entirely upon Christ and by living with the desire for some other novelty."[75]

There really isn't any way that we as humans can verbalize or rationalize exactly this great act of love from God, for God made all things and found all His work holy and good. As humans we try to rationalize God's action by comparing it to something we can understand. I really don't think we as humans can truly understand this action of God, where God the son was born of a human mother, Mary. What in our own lives can we compare to this kind of transformation from God to human? What if we changed from a human into a worm crawling through the ground? There really isn't any way to fully understand this great

---

[75] *#65, excerpt used from "Catechism of the Catholic Church," Liberia Editrice Vaticana, Citta del Vaticano, 1997, did not need written approval because I met their guidelines, (http://usccb.org)*

mystery of a son of God that was born of a woman, a child who is both fully God and fully human.

As a child of about seven or eight, as I was getting up from the edge of a canal lock from where I was fishing, going to get another worm for my hook, but as I got up I lost my balance and fell backwards into the lock, my dad without hesitation jumped into the water to grab me before I drowned, even though he was not a very good swimmer, he rescued me from a possible death, even at a great peril to his own life. Our God loves us this much, in that He was willing to place His son Jesus in the world that He created in the first place to save us from our own fallen nature.

In the movie, "Saving Private Ryan," a group of nine soldiers looked for Private Ryan deep in France during World War II, Private Ryan had just been informed that all four of his brothers had died in battle, and now he was going to be sent home from the war. In the final scene as Capt. Miller is in his last moments of his life, he tells Pvt. Ryan to "earn this," that knowing that seven of their men had died on their mission to save him. As Mr. Ryan stood before the burial marker for Capt. Miller he evaluated those words, "I did earn a good life because of the men's sacrifice, I am a good man who has lived my life the best way I can."[76] The death of these men shaped Private Ryan's whole life; he spent his whole life trying to live up to this great sacrifice of life.

Each of these soldiers went on the mission because they were ordered by their Army Commander. Jesus mission to the world was much different than Capt. Millers; he wasn't ordered by God to do this task, but Jesus came to the world out of his respect for his Father's will. One group of men came to save one son, while Jesus came to save all sons and daughters. Private Ryan was now given a chance to live out his life around his

---

[76]   *"Saving Private Ryan, 1998 film, written by Robert Rodat, directed by Steven Spielberg (paraphrased from movie, only two small quotes were used in text)*

home in Iowa, in the best way he could, based according to a set idea of what a "good' life is supposed to mean. While Jesus calls all mankind to live the "good" life, it is not a life defined by man, but a life defined by God our Father through Jesus.

"Jesus cried out in a loud voice, 'Father, into your hands I commend my Spirit;' and when he had said this he breathed his last."[77]

Our pathway to heaven is now open through Jesus because of our Father's great love for us. What will you do now? Will you accept this great act of love and begin your walk with Jesus along the narrow path? Jesus ascended back to heaven to be with his Father, Jesus now becomes the bridge or path between heaven and earth, it was through Jesus that the Father sent the Holy Spirit into the world to become a teacher and advocate for each of our lives. God through Jesus picked Peter, an Apostle to become the head or leader of his Church in the world, giving Peter the keys to the Kingdom. Can you now understand the level of love God has for us yet? Can you feel God signing Jesus' name into your palm yet? When will your "light bulb" turn on and recognize and accept Jesus' great gift from the cross? You now have the choice to follow Jesus along his narrow pathway towards heaven, or you can continue along the wide road of the world. Will God's love through Jesus be enough to give you the courage to begin a new journey with Jesus? Only you know the answer. So choose!

---

[77] *Luke 23:46, NAB*

Chapter 9

PATH TO GOD, HOLY FIRE!

*"For I will take you away from among the nations,
gather you from all the foreign lands, and bring you
back to your own land. I will sprinkle clean water upon
you to cleanse you from all your impurities, and from
all your idols I will cleanse you. I will give you a new
heart and place a new spirit within you, taking from
your bodies your stony hearts and giving you natural
hearts. I will put my spirit within you and make you
live by my statutes, careful to observe my decrees. You
shall live in the land I gave your fathers; you shall be
my people, and I will be your God."*[78]

Because of their sin, the people of Israel was often conquered
by other nations and many of the Judean people were captured and
forced into slavery and taken back to the conquering King's own
territory; this action was seen as a punishment from God. The
scripture above explains that God intended to gather His people
once again and place them back in the land He had promised to
Abraham so many centuries before. God tells us that He will
purify each person with water, washing away their impurities
in all the areas of their life. Israel, like heaven requires for each
person to be in a certain state of grace, free of sin when entering
this new land of God. Our ticket to enter the land is a pure soul,
free of sin, and so we must all take those steps to be purified.

Again we are seeing God's action in the world, God's will
for our lives, He wills that we live our lives in a certain way.
Over and over we are seeing God's action within our lives:

---

[78]   *Ez.36:24-28,NAB*

1. I will take you from these nations where you were enslaved.
2. I will gather you together and bring you home to the land I promised to Abraham.
3. That it is I that will wash away your impurities with water,
4. It is I that will turn your stony heart into a natural heart beating with love and gratitude for me.
5. It is God who sent His only son Jesus into the world born of a woman to teach us about how God loves us so dearly, but to also die for all of our sins on that Holy Cross.
6. It was because of Jesus' obedience to God, that God sent the Holy Spirit through Jesus into the world, a Spirit that can now baptize us with fire and can now transform the Apostles and the Catholic Church that Jesus established through Peter.
7. It was God's will that Jesus form the visible sign and presence of the Catholic Church in the world, and that Peter was given the keys to heaven and earth, which includes the power to forgive or hold bound the sins of the people.

It is the Holy Spirit that works within our souls to free up sin from within our lives, bringing each sin into the light of Christ, where we can be freed of the power over each of our sins, but we have to follow Jesus' advice, *"Go and sin no more."(John 8:11, NAB)* If we do as Jesus commands, then we can be sure that we are on this narrow path towards the Cross. But when we see those same sins keep coming back in our lives after every confession, then we are missing something here.

Let me share by an example: We have a woman who is sitting in prison because she was arrested several times because of drug abuse. So when this woman was released from prison, she was encouraged by her parole officer to stay away from her old friends and hang-outs. But if you don't have a stable environment filled with family or friends in that new location, then that woman would more likely still choose to go home to where she had a sense of belonging. It doesn't matter if you come from wealthy family or from a family with less money, most everyone will return home to where their friends and family are living. In many cases these folks often return to their old habits bit by bit each day. So is it any wonder that they often find themselves back in court and possibly heading back to jail.

So if it seems that if we are always confessing the same sin, we must also acknowledge that there are other sins, or life choices attached to this one sinful behavior that we don't realize that is also affecting our attachment to this one sin. What is the reason why a person would try taking a drug like cocaine? Is it because your friends or family members were doing it, and you didn't want to be left out? Is it because the other drugs you were taking weren't making you high enough? Was it boredom that pushed you towards drugs? Is there some hurt that you are trying to forget? Do you get the picture yet? Every sin has many root causes, so the Lord is telling us that we must face each cause of our sin and ask the Lord to forgive all these areas as well. Jesus will send upon us the Holy Spirit to help us root all these influences behind each of our sins.

When a person keeps coming back to confess the same sin over and over then they haven't realized something to themselves yet; that they don't have the power to change the pattern of sins in their life by themselves, they never did have the power really. That power alone was given to Jesus by his Father, because the Lord was obedient to his Father's will in everything he ever did in Israel. What is also missing from the solution that when we continually repeat the same sins over and over again, it is because we are not taking the time to pray and seek out God's will over our lives each day.

So how do we get rid of our sins? It is not as simple as being baptized by your priest or minister, nor is it as simple as going to Confession with a priest. God's grace is waiting to wash away our sins. Jesus died on the cross so that our sins can be forgiven. The Holy Spirit is given to us to help us grow in our understanding of our faith in God, and a part of that is in helping us to see the many sins that guide how we live in this world. Jesus left the world a visible Church that was given to Peter, a Church that also informs our faith and teaches us about the many truths of God. The seven Sacraments given by Jesus to the Church are special graces that unite us with God in a unique way.

God the Father wants us to be holy and pure. God the Son wants us to be holy and pure. God the Holy Spirit wants us to be holy and pure. The Catholic Church and every other church wants each of us to be holy and pure. I think I am missing somebody here, oh yea; it is you and I that now need to become a part of this solution, a solution that will allow us to leave our sins behind as we travel the narrow path to Jesus.

It is true that Baptism by water washes away our sins, especially our Original Sin that we inherited from Adam and Eve. And when we go before our priest and confess our sins, these sins are forgiven by Jesus. These two graces from God are just the beginning process for this healing process. Following our confession, the Priest will then give us a penance for us to pray, these prayers are usually directed towards the Lord, in reality these prayers become a focal point as we think about our sins and how they have changed our lives, our penance unites us with Jesus for a few moments longer before we must return to our busy lives at home. As a child I went to confession because that is what my mother wanted us to do, I received from our priest a list of prayers that we had to pray before we could leave the church. Several weeks later, my mother brought us back into the church for confessions, and I would probably report the same types of sins I had told the priest two weeks before. So, where did I fail in the confession of my sins? I imagine if you asked any priest today, he would probably say that most folks keep bringing back to him the same kinds of sins each time they come to confession. So, what are you and I doing wrong when it comes to our lack of ability for truly giving to Jesus all of our sins, especially those same sins we repeat over and over each day? Here are some useful suggestions you might want to try:

1. Really the first step we need to take is this: We need to decide if we are ready to give up our sins to Jesus. When I was a child I always confessed this one sin every time in confession, I got in a fight with my younger sister, by teasing too much or yelling at her—I didn't like my sister because I was always jealous of her for some reason. Today, my sister and I are very close, no longer jealous, but I now have a deep respect and love for her today. But the sins of a child are far different from those of an adult, so we need to spend time in prayer and reflection and think through each of these sins. But, know also, we are never alone in this task in naming our sins—for God is right there beside us at each moment, giving us encouragement, giving us strength, giving us an unconditional love, giving us his son Jesus, and giving us His Holy Spirit.

2. Pray to God and ask Him for the grace to be truly open to His son Jesus Christ's truth, and to give us a heart that is ready for a change in the way we live each day.

3. Pray to Jesus and ask him to open your eyes to see the power that we have given to these frequent sins, so we can see these same sins as the Lord does from Calvary.

4. Pray to the Holy Spirit and ask the Holy Spirit to help bring each and every one of your sins to the priest, the Holy Spirit will shed its light upon each sin, so you can truly see what harm each sin does for the world. This same Holy Spirit will also inform us of those sins that we no longer think of as being sin—they are just a part of our character or way we approach life.

5. Spend more than just a few moments before you go to confession, spend hours in prayer, even days thinking about your sins, and the effect the sins have had on your life.

6. Go to confession often with your priest, spend more than a minute in the confessional, but when there, please ask the priest for some spiritual insight into the

gravity and the power that we have often had given to these sins.

7. After confession spend more time in prayer, pray through the prayers assigned as penance by your priest, but most of all give thanks and praise to Jesus for this great grace of our faith.

8. Giving up your sins is going to be hard, and it will require you to be patient with yourself, and it will take effort upon your part. Don't be surprised if you face those same temptations within your life, for these actions have been a part of your life for a long time. See these temptations as a way to discipline your faith, just because those temptations are there before you, it doesn't mean you have to act upon those temptations. Like the Israelites in the desert these sins will eventually fade from your life and you will be truly free of these sins. But, we must also know that God's grace is always near us for the taking. Every sin has been given a hold over our lives in some way; it is something that we have allowed to happen within our lives. But, these sins have no power over Christ, so we need the Lord's grace in ridding our lives of these sins.

9. The world has many models from which we can learn how to live holier lives, most of the men and women we call Saints were sinners at one time or another, so you can read books about them, and you can see how they learned to align their will with the Lord's will, and how they dealt with sin in their lives. Most Saints took many safe guards in striving not to be placed in areas they were weak by nature, as a priest, they would never look a woman in the eye, or be in a room all alone with a woman.

God remains our Creator for all of eternity; Jesus becomes the Savior of the world. God pours out His love on us daily, whereas Jesus always points us to his Father in heaven, the Holy

Spirit coming from the Father through Jesus, always directs the person towards Jesus, and the Spirit working within the Church founded through Peter will always direct us towards Jesus. Everything that God has done has been done for our behalf, in bringing us back into that relationship we once shared with Him in heaven, a relationship that is between a Father and a child, whereas the life of the child must learn to become obedient to the will of the Father, and we must have a love that flows out of our gratitude for the life were are given through Jesus Christ.

As a teenager I worked on a pig farm, I would always wear a different set of clothes for work on the farm; so, when work was over I would change back into the clean clothes that I wore to work. Upon arriving home in my clean clothes it wouldn't take too long before I was asked to take a shower, even though I was wearing clean clothes, I still smelled like the pig farm. As God's people we have to know that something within our soul has to change before we can return to heaven, our bodies need to be purified and cleansed by the baptism of water, forgiven from the cross of Jesus and taught by Jesus through the actions of the Holy Spirit to remain free from the effects of sins on our lives. It is the Holy Spirit who becomes the words written on our hearts that can now guide our actions in life. It is the Spirit who will convict us of our sins and help us to recognize our sins impact on our lives and of those same sins in the world. The Holy Spirit always points us towards Jesus, and it is the Spirit who now becomes our guide as we travel this narrow pathway to Jesus and ultimately heaven.

It was John the Baptist who leapt in his mother's womb when Mary came to their home. Jesus first act in his ministry was to go and be baptized by John in the Jordan, and John says that he was not fit to untie the straps on the Lord's sandals. John was also a witness to hearing God announce His favor for Jesus. John went on to say that while he baptized Jesus with water, that it will be Jesus who will baptize the world with the Holy Spirit, and with fire.

"No one comprehends the thoughts of God except the Spirit of God. Now God's Spirit, who reveals God, makes known to us Christ, his Word, his living Utterance, but the Spirit does not speak of himself, the Spirit who has spoken through the prophets makes us hear the Father's Word, but we do not hear the Spirit himself. We know him only in the movement by which he reveals the Word to us and disposes us to welcome him in faith. The Spirit of truth who unveils Christ to us will not speak on his own. Such properly divine self-effacement explains why the world cannot receive (him), because it neither sees him nor knows him, while those who believe in Christ know the Spirit because he dwells with them." [79]

Growing up on my parent's farm south of Tiskilwa; as one child amongst two other brothers and four sisters we were often guided by our parent's will for us each day. From the time we woke up each day, to the types of chores we needed to complete each day, or the times we ate our meals, and the time we were to go to our bed each night. I remember one of several times where I exerted my will over my father and refused to do a task he assigned me, perhaps I wasn't done playing some game, I don't remember the exact reason, but I do remember my father's reaction to this defiance, I received discipline of several swats from a switch off our maple tree. Our parents never asked us to do the impossible or put us in great danger, but they assigned tasks according to our age and abilities: like feeding animals, cleaning hog pens, running errands, mowing grass, cleaning our bedroom or other rooms, etc., all tasks that were necessary for the basic working of the farm.

Our Father in heaven wills us to listen to and follow the commands that are necessary for the building up of His world.

---

[79]   *#687, excerpt used from "Catechism of the Catholic Church," Liberia Editrice Vaticana, Citta del Vaticano, 1997, did not need written approval because I met their guidelines, (http://usccb.org)*

Not because the commands are impossible or dangerous; but because these commands and actions are for the good of a home, or a community, or a nation, or the greater world. Like our parents, God desires that we remain obedient to those commands because they do have an impact in the world and they also demonstrate to God; or our parents a certain level of trust and respect from our part as we fulfill their will or action within our daily lives. When we look at Jesus Christ's life, it is a life lived in total obedience to both his mother and step-father Joseph for those thirty years of his life. The Lord's whole life from conception to his final breath on the cross was in doing his Father's will in all things. It was out of this obedience to God that Jesus was granted the power to judge us upon our death, as he also was given the power to forgive us of our sins. God sent the Holy Spirit through Jesus into the Church and the Apostles to help us each along this great journey, to help us to grow in our faith and trust of Jesus.

We are back in the Garden of Eden once again to revisit what happened between God the Father, and Adam and Eve. Remember how Adam was obedient to God as they named the plants and animals of the world, God created, Adam provided the name, God willed, man does God's will. Scripture tells us that God walked amongst the Garden, worked alongside man, provided all their needs for the couple, like Jesus, both Adam and Eve seemed to know the mind or will of their Father. Jesus was given to the world in order to give us a chance to know God the Father this well once again, so we can accept His will over our lives and accept our place in the world God created for us.

Prior to our own birth in this world created by God, we too once conversed with God in heaven. Growing up on the farm and working through the different stages of childhood, and on through the teenage years I had a good sense of the kind of man my father was, I certainly didn't know the depths of his mind, nor the dreams he had for his life. I saw a man who loved and guided his family through life, guiding us and encouraging us as we each grew into adulthood. He never judged, he allowed us to make mistakes, but our dad was always there when we stumbled, he was a pillar of strength when we faced several medical trials, like my mom's cancer, or his own heart health problems, or even my own struggles with my neuromuscular disease. It was during an active phase of my neuromuscular disease where I went from a man who could walk up and down hills to one who could barely crawl on my hands and knees. It was during this great trial that I got to know my parents in a much deeper way, I could see the pain and anguish they had for me as a son, and the guilt they had for their other children because so much worry and care was given to me.

We must also recognize that we can never be equals with God, for only God knows what we each must do with our lives in this world. God planted us each with certain gifts that have the potential for making the world a better place to live, with the right guidance from the Holy Spirit our lives as Christians can truly change the lives and direction of other people in our world.

God told Adam and Eve that that they could eat from all the other trees, but they should not eat from the tree of knowledge of good and evil. But, Satan tricked them into eating from this tree, saying they would find greater peace from eating this fruit. It was a bite that changed the world forever, it changed their whole lives—forever banned from the Garden of Eden, separated from the tree of life, forever placing that barrier between heaven and earth, our survival and future was now dependent upon the sweat of our brow and we as humans experienced pain for the first time in the world. They experienced for the first time shame as they hid their deeds from God, knowingly aware of their own nakedness or failings before God, but as time passed and we struggled with the many areas of life, mankind began to fail God in other areas of our life as well: murder, lying, coveting, stealing, worshipping false idols, by not honoring our parents, and by not honoring our God.

In time these sins also changed our view in life, no longer do we feel shame for these sins; and for some people these sins are as natural to us as breathing. Remember the parents I mentioned that taught their children how to fight and steal from others. These parents could not see that their actions for violence and theft as being an evil act, these sins had become such a natural part of their life. Following our expulsion from the Garden, even though we ate from the tree of knowledge of good and evil, it would seem at first having this knowledge would be good for us, in that now we would have greater moral clarity in knowing which action is good or evil, but since this act was in defiance of God's will, meaning that we ate from the tree against God's will anyway, this sin now has forever changed our ability to truly determine the difference between good and evil. Only God, who is pure, has the knowledge to determine what is good or evil for us as a people.

The very fact that Jesus remained obedient to God the Father his whole life, even taking and accepting all of mankind's sins, including our very own onto that cross. That obedience to the Father's will for the world, has turned the power from the cross into the Tree of Life, the tree that now unites heaven and earth in a similar way as it did in the Garden of Eden. The Tree of Life, the cross becomes our destination point on the narrow path to heaven through Jesus. It is because of Jesus obedience that God sends the power of the Holy Spirit into our world, for it is the Spirit who becomes our Advocate and Counselor, and a teacher of all things Jesus. The Spirit has the power to transform our lives by its actions (fire) upon our soul, it has the power to convict us of our sin, and it shows us that only Jesus has the ability for forgiving our sins and freeing us from the burden of sin upon our lives.

As a child I loved reading murder mysteries, as I grew older I began to love reading science fiction books, then I loved reading books on World or American history. Ever since I began my walk with Jesus during an active phase of my neuromuscular disease I have primarily only read books that have helped me grow in my faith and understanding of God. I also have a passion for reading news articles relating to our world and nation. I guess in many ways my interest in the world helps me to better understand the many differences there are between people all across the world, and in turn I can understand my own place in the world a little bit better. Our world is filled with countless mysteries that challenge us each to expand our view of the world. There is no greater mystery than those involving God as three persons:

1. Why does care so much about us?
2. How can a God become a human being?
3. Why God placed his son on the cross at Calvary, carrying all the sins of the world?
4. How does the Holy Spirit function within the world, but especially within our very own lives? Plus dozens of other mysteries.

I remember one time as I was saying the rosary before Mass one Sunday, I was given a grace where I felt I was taken back in time to witness Jesus carrying his cross to Calvary, I remember standing near a stairway and amongst other people, hearing all the commotions and the smells of the city filled with people and animals for the Passover, and standing with awe and wonder as to what was happening in my mind, I remember Jesus walking by, trying with his every ounce of strength for taking another step closer to Calvary, he didn't look at me but I knew this was a very holy moment for my life, and I thanked Jesus for this grace.

I am sure that most people reading this passage has seen people whose sins have changed the direction of their lives. The United States is the number one country in the world with greatest number of people in prison. Our country is the number one importer of illegal drugs in the world, as a nation we spend hundreds of billions of dollars on drugs, on alcohol, on the sex industry, on gambling, on sports teams, on the movie and television industry. Every year the violence in the streets has killed more people than those killed in some of our nation's wars. Thousands of people are committing suicide each year, because they can't face another day of pain in this world, many of them are veterans coming back from our wars around the world, bereft of a purpose, bereft of family or bereft of a nation that don't care for them anymore.

Why do we still choose to "live lives of quiet desperation," as Henry David Thoreau suggests?[80] Do we prefer living this kind of life, or is it because we don't know how to change the course of our lives, after all so many people are travelling on this wide road of desperation? Following Jesus along this narrow path is hard because it stands against pretty much every aspect of our American culture.

Growing up in the home I did and with the parents I had, I knew that my parents loved each of us unconditionally, they taught us about right and wrong, they provided for our bodily needs, they expected us to complete our daily chores and work for the common good of the family, but they also gave us the freedom to choose what sports or activities in school to take part in. Every day they demonstrated a love for their family, a love for their siblings/cousins /uncles/aunts, and they taught us about the depth and beauty of America by having us visit many national parks, or in visiting the many historical sites around the country. I was given a frame of reference for knowing what a good father is supposed to do in each family, and this frame of reference has helped me understand our Father in heaven better.

Certainly the view I have of a father; is going to be far different than a child who is growing up in a home where they were neglected, abandoned or abused physically or sexually. Is there any hope for the child born amongst such pain and hurt to understand the kind of love and direction that a heavenly Father wants for their lives?

Which child of a parent has a better chance for finding this pathway to the cross? History shows us that both kinds of families have the potential for turning children into saints.

---

[80]   *Partial Quote from "Economy" by Henry David Thoreau*

What I think we are always forgetting is that it is not through our own efforts that we find God, but that it is God who calls us out of our lives and transforms our lives into something quite extraordinary, extraordinary because it is through Jesus Christ's death on the cross that we become free of those sins, and our life is changed forever. But we still must choose to accept this grace and will for our lives each moment.

Father Lauer; said during Mass on a Charismatic retreat that if we as Christians are failing to live as Christ calls us to live out our lives, because our world has not been changed enough by our love for Jesus. How do we know that we are failing Jesus in the world? First off we can still see that sin is rampant in every corner of the world, war, violence, drugs, alcohol, theft, gangs, and the sex industry and so on. All these sins were present before, during and in every generation since Jesus was born. The Catholic Church that Jesus established through Peter is now divided into over three hundred different Catholic branches, while our Protestant brethren are divided into over thirty three thousand different denominations.[81]

God tells us in scripture that the wide road is filled with people going the wrong direction in life. We are going back again to the scene of the original crime against God the Father, where Adam and Eve were instructed by God to eat from the Tree of Life, but not eat from the Tree of Knowledge of Good and Evil. Although Adam and Eve's choice for eating from this tree falls on their shoulders because they knew they were going against God's will for them, but a portion of the blame also falls on Satan who enticed them into believing that this food would give them peace of mind since they can now be like god and know what actions are good or evil. But this one sin changed their world, just as our sins have changed our own lives and the world in which we live in today. We are born with this original sin, baptism washes us free from this sin, but it is our other

---

[81]   data taken from (http://en.wikipedia.org/wiki/
        Demographics_of_the_world)

sins that affect our ability for recognizing the different nature between good and evil acts. Make no mistake our ability for knowing what is good or evil is far different than what God knows for our lives. For instance, some people might think cussing is a normal way to speak in the world, while my mother would have washed our mouths out with soap, meaning cussing is bad habit or an evil action.

I am not in a position to speak for God, because I can't judge from the pureness of God's own understanding, because I will never be God. As a son to my father Roger, no matter what I say or do I can never become my father, in much the same way we can never become or speak for our Father in heaven. Jesus says we can be called the adopted sons and daughters of God because of his sacrifice on the cross, provided we allow this grace to purify our lives and we make it to the Tree of Life at the end of our life on earth. But our adoption as sons and daughters doesn't still make us equal to God; and certainly not equal to his son Jesus either.

As Catholics we recognize that certain men and women have lived such a life here on earth that demonstrates a life lived for and through the will of Jesus, we call them saints, we ask them to pray to Jesus for us, asking for certain favors. As Catholics we are not worshiping the saints like we worship God the Father, or God the Son or God the Holy Spirit. Most Catholics are only showing honor to these saints, and we ask them to pray to Jesus on our behalf, much like we ask for our family and friends to pray for a certain need. We know that Jesus always points us to God the Father, that the Holy Spirit always directs us to God through Jesus, the Catholic Church founded by God through Jesus also points us to Jesus, Mary the Mother of God always takes us to Jesus, and so do those men and women we call saints—they always point us to Jesus.

If we make it to heaven through the grace of the cross, and are judged by Jesus on Judgment Day, and we walk through that gate into Paradise, the angels and all the other people in heaven are not there to worship us, but all of heaven is there to worship and praise God and Jesus for all of eternity.

My point being is that no matter how pure our lives are at this moment, our own knowledge of good and evil will never live up to the standards that God places on those actions because we can never be God. Every sin we have done within our lives has affected us in our ability for recognizing what activities are good or evil for our lives. This is another reason why we will never break the patterns of sin on our own, because we have no basis to know when that sin is free from its power over our lives. Only God through Jesus has the power to break the power of sin over our lives, we have the forgiveness from the cross, we have the Holy Spirit within us that will convict us of those sins and then work within us to rid these sins within our life, and we have the Church Jesus established that is now an instrument of God's grace in the world, a church that shares these seven gifts of grace with the people of the world.

It will be the Spirit who will change our mind on righteousness as well. Today all across our country there are two political parties who each display a whole lot of righteousness, it's my way or the highway kind of attitude, that we each have no choice or say in how you will live in this world, I will enforce my will over your will because you aren't as strong as I. But this righteousness is flawed because we are flawed by the sins we have committed. The righteous anger being displayed by both parties is based on our own flawed beliefs and systems, in a way we are saying to the world that I am better, my ideas are better than yours, so you better accept my will for you. But, there is a difference between our use of righteousness and the righteousness of God. Our sense of righteousness flows from our flawed nature, because sin had changed our nature, but God's sense of righteousness flows out of His holy nature.

I want to go back to this quote from Cure of Ar's book on his life to explain how righteousness is lived out within a person's life.

"My friends, I know what you are thinking too. Of course, M'sieur Cure is a priest. Of course he disapproves of the way we live. No my friends, it is not disapproval I feel for you, I feel sorry for you. Why do I feel sorry for you? Because, my friends, I know that you are throwing away the only thing that really counts! Jean-Marie was crying harder now. What you are throwing away my friends? He cried. As if you didn't know! You are throwing away the chance of heaven! And what is heaven, my friends? You know that too, heaven is where one sees God face to face."[82]

At first glance the people believed that their priest looked down on their lives, because of his elevated status as a priest, they mistook his concern for their lives as righteousness, but it was a concern born out of his love for them as a people. This was a man who endured long hours within the confessional, sixteen to twenty hours a day, and seven days a week listening to person after person sharing their litany of sins. Like a surgeon, the Cure' of Ars had the ability through a gift of the Holy Spirit to see within the penitent's heart and bring out all the sins within a person's life, bringing them out into the light of Christ's cross where these sins could now be forgiven. The people of that village and the thousands of people from all over France and Europe who sought out confession with this humble servant were changed by this one man's righteousness, for it didn't flow from a sense of power, but the righteousness flowed out of his love for Jesus into the people he truly loved.

God's will, man does God's will was his whole message, if we could do this we have hope for entering heaven to be with God, and if we don't we will be forever cut off from God's presence, this is the flip side of God's righteousness. Man's

[82] *p.105-106, excerpt used from "The Cure of Ars: The Priest Who Out-Talked the Devil," by Milton Lomask, Ignatius Press, 1958, used with permission, (http://www.ignatius.com)*

righteousness places our will over another person, whereas they try to change the law and force people to live a certain way whether they believe in the law or not. Make no mistake that God wants us to live in a certain way also, in following His will for the many areas of our lives, but God will not force His own will over our act of free will, but God also makes it known to us that there is a consequence for our choice, one is accepting God's will through Jesus for our lives, or we can remain apart from God forever.

When Jesus cleared the Jerusalem Temple of tables and moneychangers he did it out of a righteous anger because they were defiling the Holy Temple through their sinful actions. In the movie, "Into the West," a scene depicted Quantrill's Raiders coming into a town in Kansas killing all the people, both men and women, including children, killing them out of their righteous anger because the folks of this town respected and worked alongside black Americans.[83] One act of righteousness was done to keep the Jerusalem Temple holy and pure, while the other act of righteousness was done to rid the world of a people who didn't believe in their ideas of superiority over another. One act flowing from God's pureness and the other flowing from man's corrupted nature.

God's every action in history represents an act of love from God to His people in the world, and His ultimate act was in giving us His son Jesus Christ, a world where all of our sins were taken in by Jesus and sacrificed on the cross. Understand that when each person appears before Jesus on Judgment Day; we will now recite our every sin that we have committed in our lifetimes, the ones we had already confessed and the sins we have hidden away from the world. It may seem that when Jesus took on all the sins of mankind onto the Cross—our sins might have become jumbled into all the other sins, but God working

---

[83]   *Into the West" mini-series, produced by Steve Koren and Mark Keefe, directed by Tom Shadyae, Universal Pictures, 2000 (paraphrased story and used no actual quotes)*

through Jesus knows each one of us as intimately as when He spoke to us in heaven prior to our birth in the world. God loves each one of us unconditionally, and we must also remember from scripture that God and the angels will be rejoicing when we come back to him, and vice versa, God and the angels will mourn our loss if we die apart from his love.

Why does God bother with us at all? Why would God ever care for a person like me? What kind of God even knows when a sparrow that has fallen to the ground, when was the last time we even made a note in our mind when we saw a bird fall to the ground? When God created the world and everything in the oceans, on the land and in the air—everything created was placed there for a purpose, God saw that His work was good each day, and on the seventh day He rested. During the last couple of days this one sole fly has been dive bombing me off and on all day, he was too fast for me to swat him dead, so what if we killed off all those insects in the world because they are just so pesky to us. We have thousands of companies devoted to killing off these pests. What would happen to the world if we did kill off all the world's insects? Life for many animals would die and it would impact us as well, insects are a vital and necessary part of how the world feeds itself.

One time at home on the farm after a rain, the wet rope on an anhydrous tank had dried out by the warm sun while dad was eating his lunch in the house, so when the rope dried out it shrank which meant the valve on the tank was slowly being opened on the anhydrous tank and the gas was spraying into the yard and drifting towards our home, and thus risking our lives. Dad ran out of the house and across the driveway to where the tractor and rig was sitting in order to reach and shut off this valve before it could harm or kill us in the home.

Why does God love us so much that he was willing to risk His son's life on the cross, just so we can be saved from harm from the many sins within our lives? God just loves His world; we don't have to understand the reason why He needs us, but that He does. Mankind has not been good to the world as they tried to subdue every aspect of the world; our actions have poisoned our lands, our wells, our streams, our oceans and air with chemicals that are slowly transforming our world towards destruction and death. The same chemicals that are ingested by the animals and plants we eat, or the water we drink, or the air we breathe are entering our bodies and changing us inside as well. My dad risked his life in shutting off the anhydrous tank, so no harm might come to us in the house. Our sins are slowly destroying the world, putting the survivability of the world in jeopardy.

So, again why does God care for us or cares for that sparrow falling to the ground? He cares because God is the Creator, it is His world we are destroying, and it is our sins that are destroying our future with Him in heaven. Remember the first brand new car you bought as an adult? In how you kept it clean every week, and why you always parked your vehicle far away from the store, just so you wouldn't get that first scratch or door ding. I remember the anger I felt when I seen my car get its first scratch or door ding. How could someone so carelessly scratch my pristine car, something I was very proud of as an adult? It may seem funny for us to believe this way, but that is part of our nature. God saw our world as good, something He loved with His whole being, while we saw that first car as something good because it stood for something in our lives, and it gave us a sense of pride. God loves us because He is God, every action; every grace given to the world is born out of this great love for us..

Even His act of judgment on each person is an act of love given for the world. I was spanked as a child when I disobeyed my parents, spanked out of the love my parent's had for me as their son. God's love and judgment is so much more, the threat of Judgment Day needs to drive us to live in the world a certain way, much in the same way my spankings changed my actions towards my responsibilities on the farm. God's future judgment is meant to open our eyes and see a possible future for our soul. Which road do we want to walk on during our life? We know what God wants for our present life and future with Him. We know what Jesus wants for us from the cross. We know what the Holy Spirit wants to do within our life, in cleansing the temple within our soul and bringing us to Jesus with a pure heart. We also know what the Church wants for us in our lifetime, a life loving and serving Jesus.

So, exercise your free will and pick your route. This is really a trick question. Doing nothing keeps you walking along the wide road of the world. The only choice we have really is when we choose to leave the wide road of the world and begin our journey travelling down that narrow path. God wills, world does God's will. God wills, Jesus does God's will. Jesus wills, man/woman does God's will. When we can live like this, then we can be sure we are on the narrow pathway towards the cross and heaven.

By now in this chapter you will have noticed that I have repeated the same message over and over again, this was done because it is a message that we need to hear this day, for tomorrow may be too late for us. God desires that every person ever born into the world would each come back to heaven; His love for us is this great. But, we can't come to Him laden with sins, but God covered this for us as well, by sending His only son into the world as a child, a child that one day would take upon his shoulders the sins of the world. And God's love didn't stop there either, He sent the Holy Spirit through Jesus into our lives to help us grow holy in our lives of faith and to help us to align our will with His son Jesus. But God didn't stop there either, for He had Jesus give the keys of the Church to Peter—who now becomes a part of the visible Church within the world, a Church that now shares the seven Sacraments of grace with the people, and is always pointing the people towards Jesus at the cross. God wants to see the wide road of the world empty of people; He wants them all to be on the Narrow Path to Jesus.

The Holy Spirit is given to us to help us recognize how our sins hurt the world and especially Jesus, but getting rid of our sins isn't our only task on this narrow path to the cross. It is about allowing Christ to work through us in the world, in becoming his voice, in becoming his hands and feet as we serve the people placed in our lives. It's about giving other people an opportunity to find Jesus within their lives. The Holy Spirit has a number of gifts of the Spirit and a number of fruits of the Spirit which can help us better serve the people that Jesus calls us to serve each day. We don't have to save the world on our own, but we must allow Jesus to touch the lives that God has placed in our path on this great journey.

Go back in time and think how you felt the first time you held your child, or a niece or nephew—do you remember the awe and wonder you felt for that child, the excitement, how your heart quickened by this overpowering sense of love of a child that has captured your heart in just a matter of milliseconds. Our love for God will be like this on the narrow path, your journey will be filled with awe and wonder, and there is nothing that will keep you from thanking and praising God for the love He has shown us.

CHAPTER **10**

PATH TO GOD: UPON THIS ROCK

I have never met a person who was famous; I was impressed by Pope John Paul II on television as he travelled around the world. I have seen a number of politicians who I either loved or I hated by their views in serving America. When I think of someone famous from my childhood, really three sets of people come to mind: John F. Kennedy was a leader that stood out for me because of my mother's love for him as a President, the astronauts of NASA carried my mind and dreams into the heavens, and the first musical band that caught my eye was the Beatles, I remembered watching the Beatles on the Ed Sullivan Show and seeing all those girls screaming and swooning as they were singing on the stage.

John the Baptist was such a man, he was able to draw crowds from the Judean countryside, and scripture says that all of Jerusalem came out into the desert to hear him preach of repentance from sin and to be baptized in the Jordan River. Whether the people came to John the Baptist out of curiosity or because they sought to understand the words that John proclaimed. Either way, if these "fans" chose baptism in the Jordan River, or they walked away and returned to their lives, a seed of God's truth was being planted in their mind about the need to be forgiven from sin through baptism.

Day in and day out, John the Baptist remained in the desert preaching to the crowds about sin and redemption, John didn't travel around the countryside to meet new people, but the people chose to come and see him at the Jordan River. It was the same for Jesus; he chose to seek out this man in the desert and asked to be baptized by John. John immediately recognized that he wasn't fit to untie the straps on this man's sandals, he prophesized that while he baptized with water, that it will be Jesus who will baptize the people with the Holy Spirit and with fire. John was one of the witnesses who had also heard God pronounce his favor on Jesus, and John also gave witness to the Holy Spirit's descent upon Jesus.

After the Lord's baptism, the Spirit led Jesus out into the desert where he began a forty day retreat; where he prayed and fasted to his Father in heaven. We all know this story by heart; we know that the devil tried to tempt Jesus into doing three different actions. Satan offered the Lord some bread because he was hungry, but the Lord replied, *"One does not live by bread alone, but by every word that comes forth from the mouth of God."*[84] Then the devil took Jesus up to a high place on the temple and told Jesus to jump, and because you are God's son you will be caught before you hit the ground, and Jesus responds by saying, *"You shall not put the Lord your God to the test."*[85] After that, the devil took Jesus up to the top of a mountain and promised him all the kingdoms of the earth, but that Jesus would have to bow down and worship him. But Jesus replied, *"The Lord, your God, shall you worship and him alone shall you serve."*[86]

On occasion I will watch a show named Pawn Stars on television and I am often flabbergasted when folks bring in a treasured family heirloom to the store to sell, heirlooms that have been passed from one generation to the next for a hundred years or more, selling these items for just a fun night out on the town. Our God is our treasured heirloom, our faith in God is something we need to treasure in our lives and pass on into the next generation, and our God is not something we should ever abandon when offered some shiny money or a fancy night on

---

84   *Matt.4:4,NAB*

85   *Matt.4:7,NAB*

86   *Matt.4:10,NAB*

the town. *"One does not live by bread alone, but by every word that comes forth from the mouth of God."*[87]

Have you ever prayed to God, or more like bartered with God; saying if you do this for me, then I will do such and such for you God. At my weakest when I was in my early twenties I bartered some with God over my life, to either let me die or to give me some hope to strengthen my faith: *"You shall not put the Lord your God to the test."*[88]

1. I dropped out of college because of my health, forever losing my hope for a career in electronics
2. I had lost my girlfriend because of my health issues, her father had recently died from cancer, she didn't have the heart to stay with me because of my neuromuscular disease
3. My car died at college, this was one sign of my independence from my parents that I had left, now this too was gone
4. I went from walking to using a wheelchair in a matter of months
5. At my weakest I was sleeping from eighteen to twenty hours a day
6. In my eyes my world was vanishing from my eyes, I really saw no future for me at all, so I would often cry myself to sleep begging God to either let me die in my sleep, or to give me some hope for living my life

God chose to give me hope; God gave me a burning desire to search out and begin to know His son Jesus. This was the day I truly was reborn in my life, and Jesus was that hope for a different kind of future. It wasn't a future where I sat by and let the Lord do the work for me, but it was the day I entered the narrow path towards Jesus on the cross, and I worked each

---

[87]   *Matt.4:4,NAB*

[88]   *Matt.4:7,NAB*

day towards bettering my relationship with him and with those family members I lived with at home. My disease got better with time and I worked my way back out into the community, I first pursued a Bachelor's Degree in Special Education, then I found a job as a special education teacher working with children with either severe physical disabilities, or Profoundly and Trainable levels of intellectual disabilities. Today, I am still making that effort for staying on this narrow path, and hopefully one day at the end of the race I will be at the foot of the cross with Jesus.

How many gods do we have in our lives? Which of our gods take up more of our time from our lives than the time we give to God each day? It takes really only a few minutes of reflection for each of us to identify and name several of those gods that take our eyes off of God. As a workaholic, I often have spent so much time working and serving the kids I taught each year that I had little strength left for prayer, but I had enough energy to watch several hours of television as a way to wind down. But Jesus replied, *"The Lord, your God, shall you worship and him alone shall you serve."*[89]

What do we notice about Jesus Christ from his first forty days in his ministry?

1.   Baptism by water, repentance of sin is mandatory
2.   That Jesus will baptize us with the Holy Spirit and with fire
3.   Jesus has God's favor
4.   The power of the Spirit will lead you throughout your life
5.   The importance of fasting
6.   The importance of prayer
7.   Must live by the word of God
8.   Don't test God's love for you
9.   Worship God alone
10. Serving God's will is important
11. Satan is present in the world

---

[89]   *Matt. 4:10, NAB*

12. Satan's power is mostly dependent upon our choice to
give Satan that power over our lives

Stage One: Gathering Supplies for the Church

When Jesus came out of the desert he immediately began
his ministry in sharing the Good News of God's love with the
world, three of the Gospels said Jesus was teaching and healing
folks even before he even began to gather his Apostles; Jesus
was beginning to be a man that was able to draw people to
him in great numbers, much like John the Baptist had in his
service to God. With John the Baptist the people came to him
at the river Jordan. But with Jesus, it was Jesus that came to
them wherever they lived, but Jesus still had people who came
to him because they saw in Jesus a bright light of hope. The
world seemed hungry for a message from God, a God that
was once seen as far away in heaven, but a God who now was
able to walk amongst the land: proclaiming, healing, expelling
demons, forgiving and encouraging each person into changing
the direction of one's life.

Scripture is pretty clear that it is God the Father who
prepared the men who became His son's Apostles, preparing
them for the entrance of Jesus into their life, not so much their
knowledge of scripture, but God had prepared these men's
hearts for the will and presence of Jesus. How many people
do you know who at a moment's notice would or could drop
whatever they were doing, in their case dropping their nets and
boats, and their responsibility to their family—to go and follow
a man they had never met before?

We all have heard of fans of a music group like the Beatles
who would leave their lives behind and follow the band from
city to city, just so they could remain in that special moment and
excitement of this group's music. If my wife and I left town at a
moment's notice due to an emergency in Chicago, we still would
have to pack our bags, gather our medicine and other necessary
items for the trip, we still would need to find someone to care

for our cat Tabitha while we were gone, and someone to take in our mail, and etc.. I can't imagine Peter stopping by his house on his way out of town and telling his wife and kids, I decided to leave you to fend for yourself, because this man I just met at my boat wants me to follow him and to make me a "Fisher of Men," so I will come back here when I can and see how you are doing, I love you, but gotta go, goodbye. It doesn't sound like that following Jesus was a paid position, so the Apostles had to worry about those people they left behind in their homes. How would these men provide for their family's physical needs while they were on the road with Jesus?

Scripture talks about Jesus and the Apostles staying at homes of people who were quite generous with their food, water, living quarters. Scriptures says there were twelve Apostles, plus a number of disciples who followed them everywhere, plus a number of other followers, including women like Mary Magdalene and the Lords own mother. So, God had also prepared other people as well, in opening up their homes and their food supplies to all these people, quite remarkable really. I can't imagine showing up my sister's home for a visit for a few days, but showing up with forty to fifty other people, needless to say she might take a deep breath and open the door, but know the impact of so many people is huge on a family, especially when our pockets are empty of coins to pay for our own meals. Scripture tells us that there are many people who are generous with what God has given them, and that there are folks who aren't so generous and welcoming to others.

From the very beginning of Jesus' ministry, Jesus taught God's message at several different levels of understanding, one level was directed towards the average person in his country—teaching in parables, and using language the people could understand. The other level of his teaching was given towards his Apostles and disciples at a much higher level of understanding, not because they were smarter than the others, but it was knowledge that expanded the teaching of specific truths on God's will for the world, for Jesus was preparing them for the day when he would no longer be physically present to them each day, preparing them to become the living vessel of all the teachings of Jesus. I once attended a Mass where the Priest had designed his sermon specifically for the children of the parish, breaking down the message to where a child could understand it. I think in many ways preparing this type of sermon is harder because you have to weed out the harder concepts in order to shed light on the core message of Christ. It is not because the children are stupid, but with time and prayer, these same kids could understand the very same concepts Jesus had taught his own Apostles.

When I was born in 1957, I didn't have the ability for eating a steak and potatoes, I started off with milk, eventually I moved up to puree foods, and in time I could eat steak on my own, but I had to grow up first. It is the same with our relationship with Jesus, as Jesus sees our growth and abilities he will send us into the world for some task equipped with the necessary knowledge and God's power: loving, sharing truth about God with others, forgiving others of their hurts, healing others by your touch, by teaching others about Jesus, by serving the many needs of others, by encouraging others on their journey, just like the Apostles did following the Lord's Ascension into heaven. Most of the people at that Mass loved when the Priest offered the Children Mass, because everyone could now see the Lord in his purest form.

Jesus was just one man who could travel only so many miles and preach so many sermons or heal so many people. That is why God gave Jesus those men for his Apostles, and those men and women for his disciples and friends. All these people grew to love Jesus and they believed in what Jesus was trying to do for the world. Jesus knew that he was going to die on the cross and that he would return to heaven to be with his Father, so the Apostles became the nucleus or the building blocks of the Church, a Church that could now expand farther into the world, more than any one man ever could.

Let's say you had to get a message to every person living today, over seven billion people. Could one man tell each of the seven billion people that God loves them on her/his own, without the use of electronics? So if Jesus formed his Church around the first twelve Apostles and taught them each three years worth of theology (God's Truth), how many years would it take if these twelve Apostles would then each get twelve new Apostles and then taught them for three years, and then each of the 144 Apostles would each pick twelve Apostles, and teach them God's truth for three years and so on? (12x12x12, etc) Any guesses? No! About twenty seven years to reach over seven billion people living today, amazing isn't it, less than the time that Jesus was alive on earth! It is really not a matter of logistics, it is about finding those individuals who can accept all the teachings Jesus had for the world, giving them that knowledge and experience and the power of the Holy Spirit to push us deeper into the world. Just think about it, it would take twenty seven years to reach every person alive today; seven billion people could have the opportunity for knowing Jesus in a really deep and spiritual way, seven billion Apostles.

"He summoned the Twelve and gave them power and authority over all demons and to cure diseases, and he sent them to proclaim the kingdom of God and to heal (the sick). He said to them, 'Take nothing for the journey, neither a walking stick, nor a sack, nor food, nor money, and let no one take a second tunic. Whatever house you enter, stay there and leave from there. And as for those who do not welcome you, when you leave that town, shake the dust from your feet in testimony against them.' Then they set out and went from village to village proclaiming the good news and curing diseases everywhere."[90]

---

[90]   *Luke 9:1-6,NAB*

Why do some people accept God's message of love for them and other people choose to live out their lives of quiet desperation as Hawthorn suggests? A large number of Jesus' own disciples left him, because they were expecting a different kind of Savior, a Savior that wouldn't be offered up on the cross for mankind's sins, or a Savior who becomes the living Body and Blood in which they were now expected to eat, in order to go to heaven.

Remember the Israel nation in the desert following Moses for those forty years, how they complained and desired to go back to Egypt. I think we also forget that for much of this time the Israel people lived and prospered in Egypt for centuries, but it was only when a new King came to the throne, that the King felt threatened by the people of Israel, and so he turned them into slaves, to take them away from their power and influence, making them slaves that built great monuments to his ego.

Another clue from scriptures we have is where the seeds either fall on good soil, or rocky ground. As a seed from God, some of the seeds will land on good soil, where in time the seed dies to itself and new life arises from the soil, reaching upward to the light in heaven, awaiting the water to give us new life and energy, feeding upon the power of the soil. Remember those trees growing up on the side of a rocky mountain, reaching heavenward, awaiting God's grace of water and being nourished by the soil that had accumulated over centuries in those cracks as the rocks and water captured the dust blowing through the mountains.

I like to believe that those disciples that left Jesus earlier eventually found their way back to Jesus; perhaps they needed more time for their hearts to be broken down by the wind and the grace of water. We have to believe that these once close disciples and followers of Jesus could come back to Jesus at a future time, perhaps changed by future acts of grace and the truth of God flowing into our world through Jesus.

By this time in our lives we have walked with Jesus for a number of years, and I suspect that many of us haven't accepted all of the Lord's truth for our lives and His world, for every time we sin we are in effect turning away from Jesus and returning to our old way of life, exactly like those departing disciples. We have to believe that we can come back to Jesus and be accepted through his grace from the cross once again, so we can go forward on this path towards the cross, truly beginning a new life in him. When I returned to God, I didn't do it on my own, sure I made the choice, but it was God who gave me grace after grace that prepared my heart and mind for that new beginning.

As a newborn infant I would have died on my own because I lacked the ability to feed and take care of my physical needs, I relied on my parent's love and grace as they fed me and took care of my needs until I could stand up on my feet and provide for my own needs. It is the same when we are made ready for the time of our second birth, I received grace after grace from the Catholic Church we attended: sacraments, sermons, teaching of faith, teaching on prayer as I was growing up as a young man, we had the love and grace of our parents and family, we had the love and efforts of teachers who gave us knowledge for expanding our world, we had the love and sacrifice of men and women who fought to make our world safe from tyranny, we had the love and sweat of a nation for getting the food grown on the farm and into our supermarkets, and we have a strong nation founded on a set of principles—our Constitution doesn't say, I the person of the Singular State, but "We the People of the United States." Yes, we are one person, but we are not alone in our lives of faith.

Stage Two: Upon this Rock!

I have always had a fascination for anything dealing with history. I remember reading about Plymouth Rock in history class during grade school; the rock had close symbolic ties to the Mayflower Compact, a compact which was a legal document that was written for the people settling in the New World. In my mind as a child I had always thought that this rock was huge, larger than life because of this Mayflower Compact and because of the people's great struggle to survive in the New World. Perhaps my vision of the Rock was due to a memory of an insurance commercial I remembered as a child as well, this huge jutting powerful rock along the coast. On one of my vacations up the East Coast I stopped at Plymouth Rock, to see this massive outcropping of rock, in reality Plymouth Rock is just a small boulder about the size of a large beach ball, a rock that was encased in a cage—which prevented people from breaking bits of rock off this one small boulder.

Simon, Andrew's brother was such a man, Jesus approached him shortly after his forty day fast/prayer retreat, and asked Simon to throw his fish net on the other side of his boat—remember this was after a day where Simon didn't catch any fish, so Simon was both tired and hungry; but Simon did as he was told by Jesus, and we now know the rest of the story. Simon Peter's nets were overflowing from every kind of fish. Jesus tells Simon that he will make him a fisher of men, and he asked Simon Peter to leave his life as a fisherman behind and begin a new life as one of his Apostles.

"He said to them, 'But who do you say that I am?'
Simon Peter said in reply, 'You are the Messiah, the son
of the living God.' Jesus said to him in reply, 'Blessed
are you, Simon son of Jonah, for flesh and blood has
not revealed this to you, but my heavenly Father, and
so I say to you, you are Peter, and upon this rock I will
build my church, and the gates of the netherworld shall
not prevail against it. I will give you the keys to the
kingdom of heaven. Whatever you bind on earth shall
be bound in heaven; and whatever you loose on earth
shall be loosed in heaven.' Then he strictly ordered his
disciples to tell no one that he was the Messiah."[91]

---

[91]   *Matt.16:15-20,NAB*

The Plymouth Rock represents for many Americans the beginning of a new kind of world between their God and the people of America, a solemn vow to live a certain way in the world. It is the same when Jesus formed his Church upon Peter the Rock, not any man, but a man known by God. Jesus was just one man who could only be in one place at one time, so the Apostles becomes those blocks of stone from which his Church could grow and expand out into the world. Remember the numbers from above, twelve apostles would each find twelve disciples and so on, it would take twenty seven years to reach over seven billion people, if each person taught twelve people about God. Remember when Jesus sent his Apostles out into the country by two's to preach the Good News of God's kingdom and doing those other acts of God's grace they have been watching Jesus do for several years: 1)The Apostles healed people of their physical diseases 2) The Apostles expelled demons from people 3) The Apostles prepared people's hearts for a new future with Jesus Christ.

Jesus didn't form the Church around just one man, he formed it around twelve Apostles, but Jesus did not give the Keys of the Kingdom to all the Apostles, but to one man alone, Peter, the Rock. But, we know now that Jesus did reach every person who ever lived in the world and those yet unborn, giving them their message of love, without the aid of any electronics device, but Jesus accomplished this message from the Cross at Calvary. We have this great gift offered to us from the cross, the chance to truly become a different person, if we but accept this grace into our lives. Our journey really does begin and end with the cross of Jesus, but it is the in- between parts of the journey where the Church that Jesus founded on Peter the Rock come into play.

While Jesus has ascended into heaven and sits at the right hand of the Father, it is now the Catholic Church built around the leadership of Peter that has the duty to do the same activities that Jesus so generously gave to the people of Israel and later to the world:

1. in eating of Eucharist
2. in preaching the Good News of Jesus Christ
3. in teaching the current and future generations of disciples, laying on of hands, bestowing God's power on new pastors
4. by baptism by water
5. by baptism of the Holy Spirit
6. by laying on of hands for healing
7. by forgiveness of sin
8. by expelling demons from people and places
9. by spending time in prayer
10. through the marriage covenant
11. in providing structure to the Church
12. a major part in preserving what Jesus taught was in writing the Gospels, and collecting the many letters written and shared in the first church communities
13. in providing for food and clothing for the poor
14. in providing for the needs of orphans and widows

I remember the moment in which I gave my life to Jesus in a whole new way, it was truly a new beginning, but there was so much more that needed to be done to get me to a point where I had my feet planted on that narrow path and I could look truly forward in my life, not mired in the past, or trapped by bad habits and sinful attitudes, but going forward with Christ.

For several summers in a row I took two online courses for college credit, courses that helped me understand my job better in the classroom. I had a book, the syllabus and a set of goals I needed to accomplish before I could get a grade for the class. If I wanted an A grade I needed to do a higher amount of written work, than either a B grade or a C grade. I was a classroom of one; there were no lectures, only assignments and a time frame from which I had to have my work completed. I really missed the actual feel of the classroom, other students with ideas and opinions, and a professor who taught and shared so many other insights never found in just one book. Our lives of faith need that kind of interaction with other people, we need to be challenged to work through those hard concepts and beliefs that often divide people into groups, so we need a Church that is made up of people, people that can get to know you as a friend or as a brother/sister in Christ.

Have you ever said something horrible to another person? Hurting their feelings deeply by some snide comment! I imagine all of us have done this at some point in our lives, I know I have done such an act[s] in my life. I remember asking for forgiveness from the person I had hurt. As a child I broke a window or two from playing baseball too close to the house. Even though I went before my parents and admitted breaking the window, and in asking for forgiveness from them, I still faced some consequences for this action. If mom and dad said I forgive you of this action, the damage was already done to the window. Even though Jesus forgives us from the cross, we still are responsible for our act in the world, which for me was forfeiting my allowance for awhile in order to pay for a new window. I remember one year at the school I taught there was this one boy who had totaled two brand new cars within one year, after the first wreck either/both the parent and insurance company provided the money for a brand new car because the boy expected it. This young man faced no consequences for wrecking these two cars, in fact he was heard bragging about it to his friends. Scriptures tell us quite correctly that our actions in life do have consequences; they do have an impact on the world, whether they are good or bad is known only by the Lord.

So how do we break free from such pain and hurt? God's love and continuous grace from the cross is our key to a new beginning. It was God's grace that broke me out of my cycle of hurt and anguish as I faced my major health problems as a young man. Let me name some of these graces:

1. Baptismal promise at birth
2. Baptism of Holy Spirit at birth
3. Anointing of sick and last rights at my birth

4. Eucharist—the local priest would bring Jesus to me
5. Forgiveness of sin both sacramental and from Jesus through prayer
6. prayer from family
7. prayer from strangers
8. Holy Spirit gave me a burning desire for reading the bible, and for reading books on world religions, searching for answers in my life
9. I was given the love and support of my parents, my siblings, my nieces and nephews and my friends
10. I received healing through doctors at the Mayo Clinic
11. I was blessed/cursed with a fair amount of stubborn will
12. I was blessed with parents who taught us how to fight through the obstacles of life and overcome them, and in turn be blessed by them

The Catholic Church built upon Peter became the instrument for many of the graces I received for my life; it is why I remain a Catholic today. I also have seen how the Catholic Church impacted and transformed both my mother and uncle Klaus' life, especially through the hard moments of life, their faith gave them strength to face those hard moments we all face in life.

When reading through the Gospels I am often struck with the struggle the Apostles and disciples often had in trying to understand many of the truths that Jesus was teaching them over the course of the years they were together, especially those truths that dealt with his death on the cross and resurrection. As a child I struggled with math all the way through school, but in college I took over twenty hours of math classes, enjoying the challenge and learning the methods of higher math. So, what changed for me in regards to math, for me I was more sure of myself as a man in college. The Apostles and disciples had lives they were living each day, their future was so closely tied by their choices in life, like working as a fisherman, so when Jesus asked them to change their whole direction in life, to one as an

Apostle, it took time for them to grow and learn what that new role for God meant for their lives. We have seen that the Apostles and disciples were struggling with all the truths of the words that Jesus taught them during their time together, we have disciples calling "shotgun" for being able to sit beside Jesus in heaven, we have Apostles who refused to believe that Jesus must suffer and die on the cross, and most of the Apostles were even more confused about what Jesus said about coming back to life.

My mother for the last three years of life struggled with her health, living with great pain, filled with cancer, and feeling the effects of all the awful chemotherapy sessions that took so much out of her, and then she faced a series of strokes which took more and more of her mind with each stroke. Eventually her physical care became too difficult for us at home to deal with from a medical point of view, so we placed her in the same nursing home that she once worked as a nurse. So when Mom finally died, my siblings and I were now fully prepared for her death, because we had three years to prepare for her loss. My father's passing was a different matter, he was here one day and gone the next—for he died from a massive heart attack. With my mother's death we had plenty of time to tell her of our love for her, while with my father's sudden death we each didn't have the time where we could tell him of our love for him, not even a good-bye.

I think the Apostles and disciples were really torn in half by their love and faith in Jesus, and they were still confused by what Jesus was teaching them about what had to occur before his death, meaning his suffering and death on the cross. The Apostles had witnessed several people coming back to life from death, so they had an idea of what the resurrection might mean for Jesus, but even this concept was limited by the Apostle's limited understanding. I have lost a good number of my best friends, and each day I still feel their loss, and I am sure you each have witnessed similar losses within your own life. It is possible for us to sense some of the pain and loss that

the Apostles felt after Jesus was crucified by what we have
experienced in our own life. Which Apostles are you more
proud of during Jesus final day on earth?

1. Would you choose Judas, a friend of Jesus for three
    years, still having the conviction for turning Jesus over
    to the authorities because he disagreed with him on
    some of his teachings, in a sense Judas was fighting for
    the beliefs of his original faith?
2. Or, would you choose the ten Apostles and other disciples
    who fled Jesus' side, in fear of their lives, because
    the authorities could arrest them as well, Peter even
    publically denied that they even knew this man Jesus?
3. Or are you more proud of the beloved Apostle John, Jesus'
    mother and Jesus' aunts and friend Mary Magdalene,
    because they stayed beside Jesus out of their love, it
    was through their love that they witnessed and faced the
    horror that Jesus faced on his way to the cross and his
    painful death at Golgotha. They were there with Jesus
    during that last horrible moment, that glorious moment,
    the moment that changed history forever.

Who is the winner of this contest? In reality, each of us has
done exactly what each of these groups had done within our
own lives, at different stages of our life:

1. turning away from Jesus because of a different belief,
    or because of sin
2. or were we hiding in fear and being afraid of the
    consequences for following Jesus
3. or were we standing in full view of the world—willing
    to take the consequences that Jesus experienced, while
    offering our love back to Jesus

Every four years in our country we have two/three political
parties who are seen encouraging their man/woman to become

the President of the United States for the next four years, each party has hundreds if not thousands of people who support and follow this one person all around the country, each person also knowing exactly what this women or man stands for in how they would govern the nation in the coming years. Have you ever wondered what happens to all these believers, believers who have staked thousands of hours of effort on this one person? Where do they go after their leader loses in the primary on their run for the Presidency? The Apostles and the other disciples lost their leader, their teacher, a man they believed in and staked thousands of hours of toil and effort on as they followed and served Jesus during those three short years, but more importantly they had lost a friend, someone they loved deeply. I remember my broken heart following the death of my parents; the Apostle's hearts had to be broken as well and I think they truly had a fear for their future because there pain was just too great.

I think for many people talking about death is hard, so we tend to quickly go through the scriptures relating to the trial and the crucifixion in order to rush to the excitement of Easter, this is wrong because if we are going to be honest with ourselves we have to accept our part in the last day of the Lord's life, being bold enough to stand before Jesus and place our sins with Jesus, the sins of our past, the sins of the present, and the sins from our future. Bold enough to accept the new words and truths coming from his mouth, bold enough to turn our back on our old way of living and pushing forward towards Jesus. It is a fact of life that there is both life and death in the physical realm—meaning that one day we will breath our last breath, just like Jesus, but we are also told through scripture that we each must become reborn in Spirit, a Spirit now flowing from God through Jesus, our future in heaven depends upon it.

I think many people are quick to judge the Apostles for their failure to stay by their Lord's side. I have vivid memories as a child of when President Kennedy was assassinated, I remember my mother crying over his death, there was lots of confusion over the assassination and the shifting of power to a new President, our future as a nation was shaken to the core. So, too with the death of Jesus; they too were unsure of their future because their leader was gone from their midst, we have to remember that it wasn't our necks on the line, we weren't the ones shocked by Judas' betrayal, nor did we know how well Jesus knew his Apostles, or how the Apostles knew Jesus, the Lord's own hands just a few hours before the trial had just washed and dried their feet with a towel, that is a pretty personal act of love between two friends.

Stage Three: In the Beginning

What a difference a day makes, yesterday the Apostles were fearful and in hiding, and when Jesus did walk amongst them again after he left the tomb on the third day, some of the truth of the Lord's teachings began to make sense for they became a reality for them as believers. After Jesus ascended into heaven to be with his Father, God sent the Holy Spirit through Jesus into the world, into both the Apostles and fledgling Church. After this Pentecost, did you see any fear, or lack of boldness as Peter was preaching above to the people of Jerusalem. It was the Spirit of God who turned a man once fearful, to a man who faced his life without fear, for Peter now understood everything and knew the direction he must now go, and that was doing the Lord's will in all things, in building up the Lord's Church and bringing people back to God, through the grace flowing from the Lord's cross.

We know from scripture that Jesus entrusted Peter with the keys to the Kingdom of Heaven and Earth, head of the newly born Mystical Body of Christ on earth, which was the Catholic Church. Peter's first act of business was to replace an Apostle for the vacant spot left by Judas, choosing by chance from those disciples who were following Jesus those three years, laying their hands on Mathias, bestowing God's power on the new Apostle. As Apostles, the task now fell upon them to become those living Christ's within the world, teaching others of God's truth and laws, proclaiming the Good News of Jesus unto the world, healing sickness, expelling demons from people, forgiving sin, baptizing new believers in water and anointing them with oils and the Holy Spirit. It was through their action at Mass that the people broke the bread of the Eucharist and consumed the Lord's body and blood, as directed by Jesus at the Last Supper.

At first the Apostles taught within the synagogue or out in the open, they also began to celebrate Mass in small neighborhood home churches. These churches were centers of prayer, teaching of the faith, places where people came to worship and break the bread of Jesus, plus people came for physical healing, spiritual healing, being cleansed from evil spirits, caring for both widows, orphans and the poor, collecting money for the various needs of the Church.

As the Church expanded the numbers of people leaving the Jewish faith, this action began to worry the leaders of the Pharisees, so Peter and the other Apostles and disciples began to be questioned by the ruling leaders, both local and religious, and these leaders directed the Apostles to quit directing the Good News of Jesus towards the people of Israel. The Religious leaders wanted some answers as to where the Apostles got the power to heal people's illnesses or in expelling demons from the people's lives. Peter was arrested and placed in jail, but an angel opened the gates, and Peter was back proclaiming the Good News of Jesus Christ. Gama was a wise religious priest who tried to calm his brothers down by saying this as noted in scripture: *"So in the present case I tell you, keep away from these men and let them alone; for if this plan or this undertaking is of men, it will fail; but if it is of God, you will not be able to overthrow them. You might even be found opposing God!"* [92] But the Religious leader's fears got the best of them; so Paul was sent throughout Israel breaking up Christian Churches,

---

[92]   *Acts 5:38-39, NAB*

placing Christians in prison, along with their leaders, even stoning some of the leaders, like a holy disciple named Stephen. So, the focus of the Lord's ministry was being forced outward, sending Apostles out into other lands, establishing new Churches in areas all around the Mediterranean, at first through the people of Jewish faith and then through the Gentiles. With the expansion of Christianity into the outside world; certain problems needed to be dealt with by the early Church:

1. As the Catholic Church expanded into other lands there were a number of issues that began to concern the Apostles and leaders of the Church, especially as the original Apostles were being martyred one after the other.

2. As the Catholic Church expanded into other lands where Gentiles lived, then the young Church had to work out the details for their believers, like whether a Gentile should follow many of the laws the people of Israel followed, for instance, circumcision and some dietary laws.

3. As the Catholic Church expanded into new areas, the problem of language come into play, not many would be able to understand Aramaic, but they might understand Greek or Latin.

4. And these early Churches also struggled because their faith was so young and their training was not as thorough as the first Apostles received, because there weren't any written books that laid down all these teachings.

Stage Four: Church Grows Up

It is impossible to condense two thousand years of Church history into one single chapter, for people are complicated because there is always that tension between their beliefs, their need for survival, their ability for understanding all the truths that Jesus taught to the Apostles, and the tension between the different people living and working within an area. The first three hundred years became the age of the martyr for the early Catholic Church, where the early Christians were being imprisoned, tortured and killed in full view of the world, this persecution was being done to quash the growth of the Christian faith in their lands. Plus certain doctrinal issues came to the forefront like:

1. Jesus being both God and Man
2. Trinity
3. role of Holy Spirit
4. formation of the New Testament
5. formal use of Prayer
6. different functions of the Church:
    a. Apostles
    b. Bishops
    c. Priests
    d. Deacons
    e. Teaching
    f. Preaching
    g. Healing
    h. Forgiveness of sin
    i. Providing for the widows, orphans and the poor
    j. Building Universities and schools
    k. Building hospitals
    l. Administrative
    m. Prayer development

As certain doctrines became a divisive issue for the various religious leaders within the Catholic Church, the Church would then convene what is called a Council, whereby Bishops and Priests would come together to discuss and pray over the various issues, and being guided by the Holy Spirit they would vote for the acceptance or refusal of this doctrine, let's say it was the doctrine on the Trinity, or the formation of the book we call the New Testament. The New Testament was formed after great thought, great effort from discussion, through prayer, reflection and the guidance of the Holy Spirit, thousands and thousands of hours of effort—that is how important it was to the Church leaders, Priests, Bishops, Apostles and the Pope to be of one mind and belief.

In nearly two thousand years of history the Catholic Church, the Church remains the same as it was when Jesus formed it upon the twelve Apostles and turning over the keys to Peter the first leader or Pope of the Church. They still do the work of Jesus:

1. The Priests, proclaim the Good News of God's love—at daily Mass in every area and nation of the world
2. Priests and disciples teach people about Jesus and the truths he taught the first Apostles—catechism, Grade School, High School, College, Master's programs in Divinity
3. Priests and disciples heal both the physical/mental/ spiritual lives of the people of the world—through the sacraments, through the hospitals we built, through the care of the poor, by providing for the widows and the orphans
4. Priests and disciples evangelize to people of all colors, all races, all faiths, to every corner of the world through their missionary efforts

I want to share some quotes taken from the Catechism of the Catholic Church that touch upon the seven great Sacraments given by Jesus to the Church:

1. *"Baptism: The Lord himself affirms that Baptism is necessary for salvation. He also commands his disciples to proclaim the Gospel to all nations and to baptize them. Baptism is necessary for salvation for those to*

whom the Gospel has been proclaimed and who have had the possibility of asking for this sacrament."[93]

2. *"Forgiveness of Sin: Christ has willed that in her prayer and life and action his whole Church should be the sign and instrument of the forgiveness and reconciliation that he acquired for us at the price of his blood. But he entrusted the exercise of the power of absolution to the apostolic ministry which he charged with the "ministry of reconciliation."* [94]

3. *"Healing of the Sick: Moved by so much suffering Christ not only allows himself to be touched by the sick, but he makes their miseries his own: He took our infirmities and bore our diseases. But he did not heal all the sick. His healings were signs of the coming of the Kingdom of God. They announced a more radical healing: the victory over sin and death through his Passover.[95]*

4. *"Eucharist: "At the Last Supper, on the night he was betrayed, our Savior instituted the Eucharistic sacrifice of his Body and Blood. This he did in order to perpetuate the sacrifice of the cross throughout the ages until he should come again"* [96] *"*

---

[93]   *#1257,excerpt used from, " Catechism of the Catholic Church," Liberia Editrice Vaticana, Citta del Vaticano, 1997, did not need written approval because I met their guidelines, (http://usccb.org)*

[94]   *#1442, excerpt used from "Catechism of the Catholic Church," Liberia Editrice Vaticana, Citta del Vaticano, 1997, did not need written approval because I met their guidelines, (http://usccb.org)*

[95]   *#1505,excerpt used from" Catechism of the Catholic Church," Liberia Editrice Vaticana, Citta del Vaticano, 1997, did not need written approval because I met their guidelines, (http://usccb.org)*

[96]   *#1323, excerpt used from "Catechism of the Catholic Church," Liberia Editrice Vaticana, Citta del Vaticano, 1997, did not need written approval because I met their guidelines, (http://usccb.org)*

5. *Confirmation: From this fact, Confirmation brings an increase and deepening of baptismal grace:*
    a. *it roots us more deeply in the divine filiations which makes us cry, Abba! Father!*
    b. *it unites us more firmly to Christ;*
    c. *it increases the gifts of the Holy Spirit in us;*
    d. *it renders our bond with the Church more perfect;*
    e. *it gives us a special strength of the Holy Spirit to spread and defend the faith by word and action as true witnesses of Christ, to confess the name of Christ boldly, and never to be ashamed of the Cross."* [97]
6. *"Holy Orders: It is directed at the unfolding of the baptismal grace of all Christians, the ministerial priesthood is a means by which Christ unceasingly builds up and leads his Church. For this reason it is transmitted by its own sacrament, the sacrament of Holy Orders."* [98]
7. *"Marriage: Holy Scripture affirms that man and woman were created for one another: It is not good that the man should be alone. The woman, flesh of his flesh, i.e., his counterpart, his equal, his nearest in all things, is given to him by God as a helpmate; she thus represents God from whom comes our help."* [99]

---

[97] *#1303, excerpt used from "Catechism of the Catholic Church," Liberia Editrice Vaticana, Citta del Vaticano, 1997, did not need written approval because I met their guidelines, (http://usccb.org)*

[98] *#1547, excerpt used from "Catechism of the Catholic Church," Liberia Editrice Vaticana, Citta del Vaticano, 1997, did not need written approval because I met their guidelines, (http://usccb.org)*

[99] *#1605, excerpt used from "Catechism of the Catholic Church," Liberia Editrice Vaticana, Citta del Vaticano, 1997, did not need written approval because I met their guidelines, (http://usccb.org)*

Our Catholic Church has come a long way since those first fearful moments after Jesus died on the cross. Each Apostle, disciple, man or woman who met Jesus was changed by his grace and after Jesus ascended into heaven they were given the power of the Holy Spirit, a Spirit that opened their eyes/minds to all that Jesus had taught them. So now they had become a people who were unafraid to reach out into the world and bring people to Jesus, even under the threat of punishment or death. The early Church relied at first on the oral tradition of the Apostles and the sharing of Jesus around their world, but they soon realized that those words needed to be put down on paper, thus preserving the teachings for a new generation and for providing the base of knowledge for instructing new converts to the Lord Jesus.

I can walk into any Catholic Church in any country of the world, and listen to the Mass in that nation's language and I would know by reading my own missal for that Sunday that I am reading the same Gospels and other readings that are being said in every Catholic Church in the world, we are not one million different churches doing our thing, but a Universal Church. I find great wonder and peace in knowing that on a day like today in every corner and area of the world the same voice and words of Jesus are proclaiming the same truths, uniting the world into this one Mystical Body of Christ.

CHAPTER 11

GO YOUR FAITH HAS HEALED YOU!

"During that awful moment or two, it seemed to Much-Afraid that she was actually looking into the abyss of horror, into an existence in which there was no Shepherd to follow, or to trust or to love—no Shepherd at all. 'Shepherd!' She shrieked, 'Shepherd! Shepherd! Help me! Where are you? Don't leave me!' Next instant the she was clinging to him, trembling from head to foot. 'Don't let anything turn me back. This path looked so wrong, I could hardly believe it was the right one,' and she sobbed bitterly." [100]

One of the reasons why I have always loved this book, "Hinds Feet on High Places," is that the book describes the kind of a journey we each much face as we are traveling on this narrow path to the High Places. The quote above suggests that there will come a time in our faith where we will journey alone without God, at least that is what we are perceiving, but this in reality is an important stage of our spiritual growth, a time where all believers must learn to exert their own inner convictions and continue down the narrow path, knowing and trusting the will of Jesus, even though we can't feel his presence nearby.

Jesus in the Garden of Gethsemane had his moment where he felt abandoned by God, but Jesus went forward and trusted

---

[100]   *P.173-174, excerpt used from "Hinds' Feet on High Places," by Hannah Hurnard, Living Books, Tyndale House Publishers, London England, 1986, followed the guidelines set by Tyndale House Publishers, (https:// www.tatepublishing.com)*

God that this is what must happen for the good of God's glory. The Apostles felt total isolation from Jesus after his death, they experienced extreme fear and uncertainty, but they went forward and came together in prayer, they broke bread, they didn't scatter back to their old lives, but stayed together because of their commitment to Jesus. This period of abandonment by Jesus is really a test of our faith in the Lord, it is a test that will challenge us to grow in our abilities to live as Christ calls us to live, but it will also make us a stronger Christian. This test of faith gives us each an opportunity to mature in our relationship with the Lord, so it becomes important for us to trust in God's will for our lives, even when we don't feel His presence, but we know it is the right thing to do.

As a younger son I had plenty of opportunities for watching my dad drive the tractor, sitting right next to him on the wheel well, so I knew from observing him what steps were needed for changing the gears of the tractor, or how to use the brakes for slowing down. I remember the first time my dad asked me to drive the tractor, I was nervous but I did as he asked. As a teenager it is natural for the teenager to try and become independent from their parents, working at a job, paying your own bills, working towards a future you have always wanted for your life. Becoming an adult is much like the period in our spiritual journey where we feel we are all alone on the journey; the key to any journey is not giving up on life, but pushing forward every day despite the pain and struggles of life. God will always be there for you as you struggle with the many heartaches and hardness that life often brings our way.

So what seems to us as abandonment by God; is really just a test of faith on our journey upward to the cross. We need to realize that this test of faith is a natural stage of our life following Jesus, it is necessary for us to pass this test before we can head to the High Places with Jesus as our guide. At our baptism we began this journey to the High Places; it is a journey where we are challenged to examine each of our belief systems that control how we live out our faith and how we live out in the world. Let us go back to our baptism and reflect on this sacrament and how it has changed our life, we each have crossed this river of baptism and we have begun our walk in the foothills or mountains our whole life. Ponder on all those areas of life that we would never have dreamed of, or how we have learned to spell out the alphabet of love? Take some time now and reflect on the love we follow in our life:

1. Love for God, the Father
2. Love for Jesus, the Shepherd
3. Love for the Holy Spirit
4. Love for our parents
5. Love for our spouse
6. Love for our siblings, nieces, nephews, cousins, aunts and uncles
7. Love for your pets
8. Love for friends at Church
9. Love for friends from work
10. Love for friends throughout your life
11. Love for the stranger
12. Love for the homeless, the poor, the orphan
13. Love for prisoners in jail
14. Love for people of your political party, or love for the opposite political party
15. Love for your nation
16. Love for all other nations
17. Love for our oceans and living creatures and plants
18. Love for our land and all living creatures and plants

Go your Faith has Healed You!

"As he went, the crowds almost crushed him. And a woman afflicted with hemorrhages for twelve years, who (had spent her whole livelihood on doctors and)

*was unable to be cured by anyone, came up behind
him and touched the tassel on his cloak. Immediately
her bleeding stopped. Jesus then asked, 'Who touched
me?' While all were denying it, Peter said, 'Master,
the crowds are pushing and pressing in upon you.' But
Jesus said, 'Someone has touched me; for I know that
power has gone out from me.'"[101]*

Our participation in following Jesus down the narrow path
is really a journey of faith and trust, in a sense it has power as
Jesus says in the above passage; for the woman believed if she
could just touch the tassel on his cloak and she would be healed.
We have to be very clear here, this woman didn't heal herself
with her own power, but all power comes from God through
Jesus. Even the power the Apostles used in healing people,
and expelling demons, bringing people back from the dead
wasn't their power, but it was Christ's power flowing through
them into the people. Faith is about believing in and trusting
in the will of our Lord Jesus over all the areas of our lives, and
believing that no matter what happens, Jesus is there to guide
us to the cross. We are asked by God to give to Jesus every
aspect of our life:

1. All of our will
2. All of our habits, both good and bad
3. All of our thoughts in every part of our world
4. All that we have learned from the world
5. All of our sins, and I mean everything, even the ones
    we don't want to let go of in our life
6. All of our desires
7. All of our losses in life
8. All of our memories of past hurts
9. All of our hopes and dreams for life
10. All of our current fears and struggles with life

---

[101] *Luke 8:42b-46, NAB*

11. All of our fears for the future
12. All of the loves of our life, placing our children, spouse into God's loving hands

I remember one Friday night while on retreat I was asked by Jesus to throw away all my research papers I had wrote out for my meditation the next day. For me it was like asking me to cut off an arm or a leg, you see I like to be in control, I like to be prepared, I spent nearly fifty hours preparing for this thirty minute talk. Eventually I got over my fear of giving my control (throwing away my written out speech) over to Jesus and allowing the Lord to speak through me during the next day's meditations. During the exact time I was wrestling with God over my control over whether I could keep the outline talk, or in trusting Jesus to say his words through my mouth, my sister and her husband were holding their dying daughter Emily who was just born prematurely, both were acts of faith and trust in God. I will never forget this lesson on faith, nor will my sister, both changed our lives forever.

We do have power when it comes to using faith, we have the power to believe in what God can give us, or we have the power not to use our faith in seeking God's help or direction. As long as Peter kept his eyes (faith) on Jesus as he was walking on the water he was doing fine, but when he let his fears take over he started to sink in the water. I always loved this scripture: *"He said to them, "Because of your little faith. Amen, I say to you, if you have faith the size of a mustard seed, you will say to this mountain, Move from here to there, and it will move. Nothing will be impossible for you."*[102] When was the last time you asked this mountain to move over there? Am I saying our faith is weak? No, not at all!

Have you ever met a person whose faith impacted the world? Easy answer: Jesus, Mary, the Apostles, numerous Saints are the ones that come first to my mind. Other people

---

[102] *Matt.17:20,NAB*

have the power to move you as well in your life. A tiny infant has the power to get their parents to move and take care of their physical needs, especially during the dead of the night. Even my cat Tabitha can get me to drop whatever I am doing in order to give her the attention she wants right now. I have worked with parents of special needs children who have moved mountains to get the education they wanted for their child. A National tragedy like 9-11 brought together millions of people; where literally a mountain of steel and debris was moved through many people's efforts.

From the moment God made the world, there was movement, suns and their planets moving through the heavens, constantly in movement. The sun is constantly burning up gasses and producing heat and light for our world. The planets that rotate around this one small sun are constantly moving. Our oceans and streams are constantly moving thus preserving life. Have you ever seen a stagnant pool of water? All life within that pool is dead. The heart begins to beat in the fifth week of a pregnancy, constantly beating until that person has died. We are breathing twenty four hours a day, in constant movement. Even when we are sleeping our body is in constant movement, so we have to know our faith also needs constant movement, how else can we ever hope to join the Shepherd in the High Places if we are still standing on the flat ground, we need to enter the narrow path and begin our journey up the mountain, so get up and begin your journey, for Jesus awaits you.

I am going to take you back in time again, because to understand faith we need to get it through our skulls this pattern of God in the world, really this book should have been called, "God wills, Man does God's will." Faith is just doing God's will in every aspect of our lives. Let's go back in time:

1. God wills, the earth and the sky responded
2. God wills, the land and the water responded
3. God wills, the animals and plants responded
4. God wills, Adam and Eve responded

5. God wills, Noah responded by building an Ark
6. God wills, the rain responded and a flood occurred over that area
7. God wills, Abraham and Sarah responded by moving their family to a new land
8. God wills, Israel experienced a seven year drought, people of Israel moved to Egypt
9. God wills, Moses responded by freeing the Israel people from slavery
10. God wills, David responds and is made a King of Israel
11. God wills, Virgin Mary responds by saying yes to God
12. God wills, the law responds by bringing Joseph and Mary and the baby Jesus to be born in a stable in Bethlehem
13. God wills, Jesus responded by obeying his parents
14. God wills, John the Baptist responded by baptizing with water in the Jordan, and preaching repentance of sin
15. God wills, Jesus responds by going into the desert to pray and fast forty days
16. God wills, Jesus responded by teaching, preaching the Good news of God, forgave sin, healed illnesses, expelled demons, brought people back from the dead, walked on the water, calmed the lake water, multiplied bread to feed the five thousand, every word, every thought, every touch, every breath was given because God willed it for him
17. God wills, Jesus responded by asking the twelve Apostles, even while knowing that the Apostle Judas would one day betray him
18. God wills, Jesus responds by sending out the Apostles by two's, empowering them to preach the Good news, to teach, to heal illnesses, to expel demons, to raise people from the dead, and the Apostles responded by doing these actions through Jesus
19. God wills, Jesus responded by giving the keys to the kingdom on earth and heaven to Peter, and Peter

responded by taking the keys and the power that went with the keys

20. God wills, Jesus responded by teaching the Apostles the various truths of God and about the seven sacraments of the Church, the Apostles, disciples and priests responded by continuing to use them through Jesus every day in the Church

21. God wills, Jesus is to be arrested, to be tried, to be punished severely, to be put to death on the cross, the authorities in Jerusalem responded by arresting Jesus, putting him on trial, punishing him, then putting him up on the Cross

22. God wills, Jesus responded by going willingly after he was arrested, suffering, carrying his cross to Golgotha, and dying on the cross

23. God wills, Jesus forgave the thief on the left and promised him that he would be in heaven that day, the thief responded by accepting this gift of grace

24. God wills, friends responded by burying Jesus in a nearby tomb

25. God wills, Jesus responds by making himself known to his Apostles and friends, as a Risen Lord

26. God wills, Jesus responds by ascending into heaven and sitting at God's right hand

27. God wills, his Holy Spirit is sent through Jesus into the Apostles and the newly formed Catholic Church, forever changing their lives and enflaming their hearts to love and serve Jesus in the world

28. God wills, Peter and his Catholic Church respond by continuing the work of Jesus in the world, which is teaching people how to live their lives of grace as they handed their lives over to God, so we can learn to accept God's will for our lives

29. God wills, that each soul being born in his world should come back to him in the future, that each of our souls are to come to him through his son Jesus Christ, that we are

to live lives of faith in serving our Lord's will, even if we were born to parents of different colors, to different nationalities, to different economic backgrounds, or different religious backgrounds, or different lifestyles, or different intelligence levels, or different emotional levels. God doesn't will only a certain number of souls return to Him, but all souls

30. God wills, that you and I and every other person in this world must search out and find this narrow pathway to Heaven, which leads to Jesus Christ at the cross. Our path is narrow is because we must travel it alone, we are one soul, one son or daughter, one mother or father, one aunt or uncle, one friend, one niece or nephew, one cousin, one co-worker, one husband or wife. The pathway is narrow because it was made by one man alone, Jesus Christ

Seven People, Seven Journeys!

I want to share seven journeys with you, for you to reflect upon, three from scripture, and four from our world today, all born under different circumstances. We know that God loves us each unconditionally. As human beings we tend to judge people by their actions or lack of actions, based in part because of our own circumstances and life choices, and our own beliefs. My hope for you is to learn there is a difference between our own judgments and what God judges in the world, our judgments are imperfect, God's judgments are perfect and just and we need to learn how to look through our Lord's eyes and understand the depth of his love for us all, even those people we have judged wrongly by our own sense of standards.

Journey One: The Officer in the Roman Army

We have an officer who is very familiar with giving and taking orders, since he was a soldier in the Roman Army, who occupied all of Israel during that period of time. We really don't know if the man had any form of faith, we do know that the man thought enough of Israel's faith to help build a synagogue church. This soldier sent some elders of this church to go and ask Jesus to come to his home and heal his slave, who was near death. Jesus responds by following the elder's directives, but the soldier seeing that Jesus was near, came out and met him on the road, and says, just say the words and I know my slave will be healed, as a soldier I say words and the task is done, so if you say the words I know it will be done. Here we have a Roman citizen, who was a member of the most powerful army in the world; a man who took orders from his superiors, and gave orders to those men underneath him. *How would Jesus judge this man upon his death?*[103]

Journey Two: An Orphan in Korea

I often listen to you-tube music while I am working on the computer, or writing out new chapters, one day this selection came up in the menu for you-tube, it was a clip from the Korea's Got Talent Show, about a young Korean man who had quite the story, a story that touched everybody's hearts, including my own. Someone had transcribed the dialogue into English, so I could understand the message of his life.

The boy's parents were killed in an accident when he was three years old, he was then sent into a foster care home, at the age of five he left the foster family and began to live on the streets. Other adults took advantage of him, using him to sell things like fruit, gum or candy bars, and for his work he got a little bit of the money to help him survive another day. The boy said he never had the chance for going to school, but talked about taking a proficiency test at the high school level, and passed. The judges asked him how he got involved in singing, he said on one night he was working in a night club and heard

---

103   *Luke 7:2-10, NAB*

this singer singing songs from an opera, the boy was struck by the earnestness of that man's voice and the beauty of the music. From that time on the boy began to sing all the time, he said it made him happy, it uplifted his spirit, it gave him purpose. The boy sang an Italian opera song perfectly that night, received a standing ovation. Several of the judges I believe wanted to take this boy under their wings, to help provide a stable home and to give him further lessons on voice. (www.youtube.com/watch, Koreas Got Talent, Sung-bong Cho is the boy)

If the boy died tomorrow, how would Jesus judge this young man, born in a once communist country, now democracy, orphaned at the age of three, always being used by the adults on the street, his path was lonely, hard, and fraught with all kinds of dangers, but he found that the music he heard and sang gave him hope for his life. By the time he finished singing on stage, every heart was weeping out of love and compassion for this young man. *How would Jesus judge this boy upon his death?*[104]

Journey Three: Woman healed by a touch of a tassel

We have a woman through no fault of her own, was hemorrhaging for years, a hemorrhaging that often set her apart from others by law. She had tried to find help from local doctors, but was never helped. I think by now the country was abuzz with this man Jesus, who has been healing many people of their illnesses and disease, so I think out of modesty this woman approached Jesus, not to communicate her need out loud, because it might seem scandalous because of the nature of the hemorrhaging, but she believed that if she could just touch a piece of the Lord's clothing that she could be healed of this affliction.

We know the woman just didn't just sit by and accept her fate, but she sought out help from doctors, and now she sought out Jesus, chased after Jesus just to touch his cloak, not his

---

[104]   *Youtube, The Homeless Boy, Korea Got Talent, 2012*

hand, not his shoulder—which would have been common on a busy street. For this woman, touching the tassel was an act of faith and God through Jesus responded and she was healed. Jesus knew right away that God's power had flowed through him and his clothes into someone around him. So, why did Jesus demand to know who had touched him, his Apostles said the street was crowded, but Jesus demanded not so much because it would embarrass the woman but as an example of a faith being lived out in the here and now. Jesus says it was your faith in him that saved her, but it was Jesus that healed her of this affliction. *How would Jesus judge this woman upon her death?*[105]

Journey Four: A Child of the Sex Trade

I just heard the story of this young woman on a national news show on television, she was one of two women who worked with an organization that helped prostitutes turn from their life and begin a new life away from this industry. One of these two women told her story as to how she became a prostitute, it began for her at age three when her dad beat her and then raped her, and then he sold her into the child sex slave business, a business that is growing in the United States and throughout the world. Under the threat of death and physical beatings from her owners, this child, this young girl, this teenager, this young woman lived a life that is unimaginable to most every person, living in fear, being raped over and over again because of some man's sexual desire.

She talked of how other people, both men and women judged her and looked down on her for being a part of something so vile and disgusting. She was treated by these upstanding people in the exact same way that her rapists had for years, with the same contempt and hatred, they saw her as a non-existent slave. She never asked to be raped by her father, or sold into the sex

---

[105]   *Luke 8:40-48,NAB*

slave business, she lived day-by-day in fear, doing an intimate act that by now had ripped out her heart and soul each day, living her life with no sense of love, she had no childhood, but she made it to the next day, and then the next. *How would Jesus judge this woman upon her death?*[106]

Journey Five: Four Men and a Man on a Stretcher

The young paralytic man was being carried by four men, they had heard that Jesus was back in the area and teaching within a home, there were a large number of people both inside and surrounding the door, so any hope of getting through the door would have been problematic, so they developed a plan and decided to get their friend to Jesus through the roof of this home, which required that a part of the roof had to be removed, certainly this action came to the notice of Jesus the moment the roof was being removed, but Jesus kept preaching and waited until the man was lowered to him on the floor. Faith is like that though, for it requires effort on our part, seeing it through until the end, and then Jesus will respond with his action, in healing the man of his paralysis. Jesus said something curious, your sins are forgiven; pick up your mat and leave. Was this man healed because of the faith of his four friends or because of his own faith? *How would Jesus judge these four friends upon their death?*

How would Jesus judge the paralytic man? We really don't know anything more about these five individuals, but we know they needed to come to Jesus if their friend was to be cured. They could have said excuse me, can you come out here Jesus and heal my friend, or they could have waited a day and brought their friend to Jesus while he was outside, but I think the story is more than that because of the unusual nature of the story, it is a story that is easily remembered by all who hear it, because it is a story of love for a friend, a love that took a lot of effort to

---

[106]   *A child sold into sex trade by her father, USA--television clip*

accomplish, faith requires effort, it is moving from one point to the next. Because of their faith, Jesus healed their friend; the friend responded by picking up his mat and left the house to go home.[107] Every year across our country millions of people are abusing alcohol or addicted to a wide variety of drugs, every day we see or know people who are "paralyzed" by their addiction to these drugs, touching every level of income in our country. I have worked with students who become paralyzed with fear once they leave their home, afraid of the many changes of their personal schedule, or in being challenged to learn new things about our world. I had a friend in college who was paralyzed by fear of the unknown; he committed suicide because he was tired of facing those fears every day. In a sense I too was paralyzed at one time by the extent of my disease, I had lost in my mind everything I had wanted in life, I remember begging God to let me die, or to give me some hope to hold onto, and God gave me Jesus, and my life was changed, I didn't stay mired in my pain, but I got up, picked up my pallet and left the house

Journey Six: A Man Named Steven

This is a story of a young man I had only known for one hour, I had just graduated from college, and I enrolled in a class so I could be certified to teach in a different state, and as a part of the classes' requirements I was assigned to work in several classrooms for a few hours, so I met Steven for the first time, he was a young man of eighteen years old, the size of an infant, non-verbal, severe mental abilities, he needed the same full care as any infant would each day. He had these beautiful blue eyes, and a smile that would charm your socks off, he loved to be held and talked to, whether it was listening to a book being read to him, or just in listening to the words coming out of your mouth. He didn't have the ability to tell us if he was hungry, or

---

107   *Mark 2:1-12, NAB*

when he needed to be changed, so he was kept on a tight daily schedule. Since I was just a volunteer I never did know about his home life, or where he lived outside school.

But Steven touched my soul, and I have never forgotten his beautiful blue eyes, or his smile, I truly believe these souls are pure gifts from heaven, born to show the people of the world how we are to live in God's world, with a complete love and trust, these folks are the Master Teachers of the world today. Every day for these children becomes a walk of faith along the narrow pathway, always moving, always striving to do the best they can in life. *How would Jesus judge this man upon his death?*

Journey Seven: I need you now to answer these questions as best as you can below, it is not a test to be graded on, but a tool to help you see how God has been working within your life.

Your Name: _____

Parent's names / Care giver's name: _____

How did they treat you? _____

_____

_____

_____

Sibling's names: _____

_____

How did they treat you? _____

_____

_____

_____

What did you like about school? _____

_____

_____

_____

What did you hate about school? ——————————————

————————————————————————————————

————————————————————————————————

————————————————————————————————

Describe your dreams, or what you wanted out of life? ————

————————————————————————————————

————————————————————————————————

————————————————————————————————

Describe your friends. ——————————————————

————————————————————————————————

————————————————————————————————

————————————————————————————————

Describe a painful moment in your life? ————————

————————————————————————————————

————————————————————————————————

————————————————————————————————

Write down one time that God touched your life. —————

————————————————————————————————

————————————————————————————————

————————————————————————————————

Write down one time that Jesus touched your life. ————

————————————————————————————————

————————————————————————————————

————————————————————————————————

Write down one time that the Holy Spirit touched your life.

————————————————————————————————

————————————————————————————————

————————————————————————————————

Write down one time where Scripture opened your eyes to a new truth. _____

_____

_____

_____

Write down one time where your Guardian angel protected you from harm. _____

_____

_____

_____

Write down one time where a Priest or pastor opened your eyes to God. _____

_____

_____

_____

Write down one time where a Sacrament opened your eyes to God

_____

_____

_____

Write down one time where you parents pointed you to God.

_____

_____

_____

Write down one time where your sibling pointed you to God.

_____

_____

_____

Write down one time where a friend pointed you towards God

_____

_____

_____

_____

Write down one time where a stranger pointed you to God ___

_____

_____

_____

_____

Where do you experience peace within your life? _____

_____

_____

_____

_____

What kinds of prayer do have with Jesus? _____

_____

_____

_____

Take some time and pray to Jesus, thanking him for his presence in your life, and especially for his gift from the cross. And then ask him this question: *How would you Lord Jesus judge me upon my death?*

If you could do this activity for a complete stranger you never met before, than certainly you can do it for Jesus every day, and Jesus will say to you, "Get up and go, your faith has healed you." Our lives in this world do matter, otherwise our God wouldn't have put us in this world at this specific time and place, in a particular country, in a particular race or color of skin, in a different array of faiths or none, born to a specific set of parents. We matter so much to God, that He was willing to sacrifice His son Jesus Christ on the cross of Calvary, so that we each could have a chance to find our way back to heaven on this narrow path. God doesn't want us to sit on our hands, or become lost in a variety of sins, but to live a life of faith worthy of His son Jesus, pushing up that slope, always moving forward in hope and struggling to overcome the pains and fears of life, trusting Jesus more each day as we consume our daily bread, but especially in trusting Jesus during the hard times, in time we will finish the journey to the cross and gaze into the eyes of the Lord and cherish his beautiful smile, but until then please stay on the narrow path until we have reached the destination that God desires for us.

I had wanted to end this chapter and book with a quote from "Hinds Feet on High Places," about when Much-Afraid reaches Jesus at the High Places at the end of her journey, to tell you of the words of the Shepherd and the love Jesus had for her, but I won't. I want you to push forward in your lives of faith, working your way up the mountain throughout your lifetime, following your path until you reach Jesus at the cross, then you will hear his words as he is standing before you, welcoming you into a brand new life, so get off your duff and ask Jesus the Good Shepherd to show you where to begin, and begin those steps to the High Places, where Jesus and God awaits you with open arms.

CHAPTER 12

CONCLUSION: FOLLOWING JESUS ON THE NARROW PATH TO GOD

"Now there was a Pharisee named Nicodemus, a ruler of the Jews. He came to Jesus at night and said to him, 'Rabbi, we know that you are a teacher who has come from God, for no one can do these signs that you are doing unless God is with him.' Jesus answered and said to him, 'Amen, amen, I say to you, no one can see the kingdom of God without being born from above.' Nicodemus said to him, 'How can a person once grown old be born again? Surely he cannot reenter his mother's womb and be born again, can he?' Jesus answered, 'Amen, amen, I say to you, no one can enter the kingdom of God without being born of water and Spirit. What is born of flesh is flesh and what is born of spirit is spirit. Do not be amazed that I told you, you must be born from above.'" [108]

God did something incredible for the world; He reunited heaven with earth again, by sending His very own son Jesus into the world through a holy and pure woman whose name was Mary. An infant who was both a child of God and a child of a woman, both God and human, a child destined to become the pathway back to God our Father. Following Jesus on the Narrow Path to God is a journey we must take part in each day, putting one foot in front of the other until we have reached the end of our journey here in this world.

---

[108] *John 3:1-7, NAB*

It was God who had placed us into a specific time and place in the world for us to live, to a specific set of parents, a specific color of skin, born into a certain nationality, raised within a certain religious belief system, or raised within a certain wealth level, or born with a certain intelligence level, or born with a certain health level, etc. I have shared many of the reasons as to why there are so many different kinds of people in the world, but I have also shared with you as well what unites us as a people of God. It is God's love that interconnects us with the other people within our part of the world, so much so that we become a part of this greater and much grander beautiful puzzle with over seven billion puzzle pieces.

Have you ever looked at a puzzle after it was completed from a distance? The lines of each individual piece are no longer visible at a distance—no longer are we individual pieces of the puzzle but we now belong to this whole and complete puzzle, or as our faith has taught us, the Body of Christ. When working on any puzzle, the first thing I do is to put the end pieces together, for in my mind having the edges of the puzzle in place, allows me a better chance for putting all those other pieces of the puzzle in their place. God has given to the world those individuals who become the edges of this great puzzle, individuals whose faith and knowledge have both shaped our faith and informed us of our purpose in the world. It is God who made us all different so that we could have an opportunity to learn and be blessed by the other people in our lives.

I was formed into the man I am today by these graces: 1) God formed me through the love of my parents, wife, students, friends and family 2) God formed me through the knowledge I learned in Mass, Catechism and school 3) God formed me through the physical struggles I have faced within my life, and the heart aches of losing loved ones. I wasn't given a brain like Steven Hawkings so I could understand how the universe worked, nor was I given the ability to lead men and women into combat, nor was I given a body that could play basketball for the Boston Celtics. Every person has those people that have helped form us into the person we are today—these important people become the edges of this great world puzzle created by God.

When Jesus was teaching the truths of God to the world he taught at two basic levels of understanding:1) the full and complete teachings he shared with his Apostles and disciples 2) Jesus taught the everyday folk using language and parables that the common person would be able to understand. In the same way God calls out two types of individuals who will serve His will in the world, and complete those tasks in building up His kingdom in the world: the Master Teacher and the Disciple:

1. Master Teacher: is a man, woman or child who perfectly reflects God into the world, a person who is able to align their will with the Lord's will. Jesus Christ is our ultimate Master Teacher, for it is his life that we each are called to follow on this narrow path to the cross. Everything Jesus had ever said or did within his life was related to following his Father's will from heaven.

   a. The Holy Spirit was given to us by God the Father through Jesus; the Holy Spirit is a Master Teacher that both inform our faith and intellect about Jesus Christ. The Holy Spirit will always direct us towards Jesus at the cross. And when we pray to God it is through the action of the Holy Spirit within our soul.

   b. The Catholic Church that Jesus founded on the earth through Peter. The first twelve Apostles became the foundation for the Church that Jesus established in the world, a Church that is now called to preserve the Good News that Jesus brought into the world, a Church whose sole mission in the world is to reflect the love and actions of Jesus into the world, a love and action that directs its people to Jesus at the cross.

i.   The Bishops were called to lead this Church by their love for both Jesus Christ and the people of the world. The Bishops are called to share the knowledge given to them by Jesus Christ. Our God calls only a few people to this level of responsibility—for it is a great task in leading all people towards the Lord. Pope Francis is not only a Bishop of our Catholic Church, but he is a Bishop for every man, woman and child of the world, for the people from every country, every color, every faith, and a Bishop over both the sinners and saints of the world.

ii. The Pastors and Ministers in our home town churches are also set aside by God because they were called by Jesus to serve and love the people within their church and community: 1) Through the teaching and witnessing of the Gospel 2) Through the prayers they offer for the people they serve 3) Through their gifts of healing broken lives 4) Through the sharing of God's sacraments with the people they serve.

iii. The Virgin Mary who is now our mother becomes that shining example of a perfect love shown to God, a woman who had accepted and followed God's will her whole life, a woman who lived her whole life free of sin, a perfect vessel for the Son of God to be formed within her womb for the greater glory of God.

iv. Joseph and the thousands of men, women and children who were called by God into the world to stand apart from others in the world, we call them Saints. It is through their lives that the rest of the world is taught how to accept the will of Jesus in their lives.

c. Those children and adults who have been called to live out their lives free of sin due to their severe physical and intellectual disabilities, a man like Steven who I had held once in my arms as a young man, a man who had lived his whole life dependent upon the love of God for his every need. These holy children are placed in every town and neighborhood in the world to be that sign to others of God's continued love and grace. These people are the world's greatest treasures because their love and pureness teaches us each about the mysteries of our God; their presence in the world brings us to the foot of the cross. Make no mistake about this—these holy children and adults are set apart from the rest of the people within the world by God, and so the message they are called to share with the world is a message that the world needs to understand and learn from, a message that will strengthen our own faith and deepen our understanding of God.

2. Disciples are those men, women and children who have been called by God to accept Jesus Christ's invitation to follow him throughout their lifetimes, to accept his invitation to enter the narrow gate and begin our journey down the narrow path to the cross. The majority of the 2.3 billion Christians living today are called to take our places as the Lord's disciples—in serving his will within the world we live each day.

Solomon was called by God to take on the role as King of Israel, and one task that he was given by God was to build Israel a Great Temple in Jerusalem, but this Great Temple was built with the sweat and efforts of the slaves and people of Israel. So, too with us disciples for every generation—we are called to do the grunt work of the kingdom and help build up the Lord's kingdom by our sweat and our own efforts.

There is no shame in being a disciple of the Lord, in allowing Jesus to work through you in the world you live. My father during WW II—took orders from the Sergeant in his squad, who took orders from his Lieutenant, who took orders from his Major, who took orders from his Colonel, who took orders from his General, who took his orders from the Commanding General, and who took his orders from the President. Each one of us are placed in the world by God for a specific purpose, which is to love and serve His son Jesus Christ, and if we are called to live and serve the people within our own small part of the world as a parent, or a teacher, or a worker at Burger King, or as a electrician and so on—then we are blessed in knowing our place in the world. But know this—as you grow in your understanding and faith in Christ, God may call you to take on more responsibilities.

Do you remember the quote from the Cure' of Ars about the state of the Ar's parish when Jean Vianney first arrived there at the start of his Priesthood? The church had been abandoned for years; the people of the community had pretty much forgotten there was a God; sin was rampant within the area. In many ways much of France was lost because the government had banned religion from within their country; so the priests went into hiding and were secretly holding Mass amongst those devout Catholics who remained inside France, like Jean's parents. When Jean came to Ars there was much work to be done. Both the church building and the people needed to be cleaned and repaired through God's grace. The Cure of Ars set about this task by reflecting Jesus back into the lives of the people of this community. At first the people were skeptical about their new priest—they saw his words in his sermon as being too righteous and coming from a highly educated man, but in time they recognized that Jean's love for them was real and was paid for with a heavy physical price.

The town of Ars in a few years had been changed by this one man's faith in Jesus, no longer were there places in town where sin could be sewn, the church was expanded in size to accommodate the larger number of people attending Mass, an orphanage was started, as was a school. God called Jean to serve the people of Ars, the people of Ars responded to God's invitation to join His son Jesus on the narrow path, so together the community was forever changed by the grace flowing from God into the world. The Cure of Ars was made a Master teacher because he allowed Jesus and the Holy Spirit to work through him as he served the people of Ars and the surrounding country, and these people in turn became the disciples in whom the Lord's love can now be reflected back out into the world.

It is Time to Leave the Wide Road of the World!

I remember as a child hunting for those three puzzle pieces that were missing from the puzzle, a puzzle that was nearly complete on our kitchen table, we searched the floors and couches because the puzzle just wasn't complete or perfect in our eyes because of those three missing pieces. Jesus came into the world to help bring back those souls lost to God. God too wants His grand puzzle to become complete and perfect; we are told that God and the angels rejoice when lost souls can find their way back to heaven through Jesus.

Only God has the ability to bring together the people into this grand puzzle because He has the advantage of being our God and the Creator of both the heavens and the world we live in today. God created us each within the wombs of our mothers and infused each of us with a soul that He breathed into our physical body, a soul that now yearns to return to God some day. God sent His son Jesus into this world to find the missing pieces to this grand heavenly puzzle. What parent doesn't worry over that child who has lost their way in the world and who is now struggling to survive in this world? Is your love for your child sitting in prison, or lost inside a world of personal pain and anguish—any different than the love you have for your other good children? Isn't the focus of your many efforts always being directed towards helping to bring that child back home to you? We are given many examples from scripture where we are told of God's great love for His people, especially those that were lost, finding that lost jewel or coin, or leaving the ninety nine sheep and looking for that lost lamb and watching for that Prodigal son to return home to you.

We know that Jesus was given to the world to save every man, woman and child from their sins—not just those people who call themselves Christian, but all peoples of every color and nation in the world, which includes people from every faith, or no faith at all. In today's world Christians number about 2.3 billion people, which also means that the remaining 4.7 billion people were placed into the world with a different faith. Did God make a mistake? I don't think so, for these 4.7 billion people are also very precious to God!

I truly believe what Father Lauer told us at that Mass while on retreat—that if every Christian actually lived as Christ called us to live in the world: 1) There would no longer be any need for war 2) All the people would have food to eat each day 3) There would no longer be murder, rapes, and theft against another person, and the many nations of the world would now serve one another in peace.

Don't you want to see a world like this for yourselves or your children today? I truly believe that God wants this for His world, it is the world where Adam and Eve lived, a world where our human will is aligned with God's will. I never got angry with my parents because I received a punishment because of some disobedience I had shown them as a child. In truth, I learned to align my will with my parent's will not because I feared the switch from the tree—but I gave them my will out of my love and trust for them as my parents. When the Prodigal son came home to his father, the father didn't berate him, nor did he punish the wayward son, instead the Father showered him with love and threw him a banquet of celebration, an act that restored the lost son back into the rightful place in the family.

Scripture tells us that if God notices every sparrow falling to the ground within the whole world, than you and I can also be sure that God knows each one of our pains, and struggles within our lives. We humans have always thought the world that we lived in truly belonged to us, to do with it as we pleased; actually our world has always belonged to God because He is the Creator of both our little world and the immense universe that lies above our heads each day. Actually our relationship with the world could be likened to one as being a visitor, relatively, we only stay in this world for a short time; where we walk on the land that God created, drink the water that God provided, breathe the air that God provided, work or capture the food that God provided for us to eat, make the clothes from the material that God provided for us to wear on our bodies. For the most part only God knows the day of our death in this world, my mother lived for fifty three years, my father lived for sixty one years, and my niece Emily lived for three hours, and over twelve of my students died before they were twenty years old. We are given to the world for a short time to spend our time pointing others towards Christ and ultimately God. No, we are really just visitors to this world made by God—placed in the exact time and place in the world that Jesus needs us to live out our lives, in service to his will.

Our world with God was not complex when Adam and Eve first walked with God in the Garden of Eden, for their will and minds were united with God's will. Adam and Eve fully recognized that God was both their Creator and Master over their lives; and that God deserved to be loved and honored by how they cooperated in doing God's will within the world they lived. Our world became much more complicated when Adam and Eve decided that they wanted to be more like God, so they ate from the Tree of Knowledge of Good and Evil—because they wanted the ability to choose for themselves what action was considered pure or evil in the world. But, this one act of defiance forever corrupted our ability for being able to choose which actions are sinful and which actions are pleasing to God.

I have seen throughout my lifetime a great struggle between people of faith and the world we were born into—a struggle that at times may isolate us from those other people who don't think and act like us. I have described many of the facets of our life in America, both the good and evil sides of our society. If we are to believe Father Lauer's teachings about our failure as Christians to align our will with Jesus—we have to assume many Christians today are not fully living out their discipleship perfectly in service to Jesus. My dad and many others had recognized the hypocrisy of many folks who had called themselves a Christian. This book is not being written for the man and woman who are already living their lives on the narrow path, but it is being written for those Christian folks still trapped on the wide road of the world.

Every person ever born is surrounded by those people who have the potential for making a profound impact on how we see and understand the world, both for the good and for the bad. Each of us will have those people that can shape our lives of faith in God. Every child, every person, all life on earth, the stars and planets in the heavens all point us to God our Creator. Jesus was given to the world so we too might live to be that reflection of God's love into the world. I don't think that there isn't a person in the world who never wonders about God, about wanting more out of their lives, nor wonders what happens to us after our own death. God our Father placed Jesus in the world to help each person to find their place in the world, and to get from where we are now in our lives and to where God wants us to be in this world, we must detach ourselves off the wide path that the world has placed us on, and follow the singular narrow path to Jesus at the cross of Calvary. There is a deep yearning within us to return to that love and peace we once experienced with God before we were born in this world, it is this yearning which pushes us on in our journey through life despite the daily pain and struggle we often face.

Each one of us is born with a free will, the ability to choose the course of our lives, whether it being the narrow path towards Jesus at the cross, or in choosing the wide road offered by the world. Jesus never forces his will over your will; Jesus wants us to accept his will for our lives based on our own love and trust of the Lord. Much of the political division we see today in our Congress is the battle between forcing a party's will over the will of the other party, and this political rancor between the two parties has only divided the people against each other. Again, Jesus came to the world to bring the people back to God, to teach the people how to align their will with God's will, and to teach us how to love and respect all peoples.

First Step: Recognition of sin and the acceptance of God's call to be reborn again in Christ

Jesus didn't tell the woman about to be stoned by the villagers that she was a sinner and deserved to die for her sins. The Lords first statement was directed towards those men who had judged her and was ready to kill her, giving them permission for throwing the stone only if they were free from sin, so when the men left the women, Jesus told the woman to get up and go and sin no more. This is the beginning step of our journey on the narrow path, it is important for us to be able to recognize our sins before Jesus and ask him for the forgiveness of those sins.

Second Step: Building that relationship through Prayer and study of Scripture

The first act that Jesus did after his baptism in the Jordan river; was to go on a forty day fast and spend time in prayer with his Father in heaven. Jesus reflected perfectly his Father's will in the world because he spent so much time in prayer with God. The one common characteristic of every saint is that they were people who spent a great deal of time in prayer each day with Jesus—they knew his voice perfectly, much like we could never forget our own parent's voice. Jesus tells us that we must come to him in prayer, away from other people and free of those other distractions. Can we call someone our friend if we haven't spoken to them in thirty years, we must be diligent in our prayers and try and pray every day to the Lord. How else are we ever going to be able to recognize his voice if we don't take the time to hear his voice?

For much of history since the Lord ascended back into heaven the people primarily listened to the Word of God as it was being proclaimed at Mass each Sunday, and through the oral teachings of these scriptures when shared in these sermons during Mass. But with the advent of the printing press the bible today can now easily be found everywhere in the world. So shake the dust off your bible and open it and begin to read the words within this book, there are words in this book that will change your life forever.

Third Step: The Importance of Church, and why we need to be there!

Many times I have read over the years about the declining number of people going to church on Sunday, both Catholic and Protestant. Why are so many folks leaving the church and re-entering the wide road of the world.

1. Poor instruction on faith
2. Too much prayer
3. Too little prayer
4. Services too rigid
5. Services that are too lax
6. Preaching is bad

7. People aren't friendly
8. People are too friendly
9. People are too judgmental
10. People could care less about you
11. Too much scripture
12. Too little scripture is being used
13. The church is too extravagant
14. The church is too plain
15. I am not being fed
16. I am not being entertained enough
17. "These pillars of the church don't act like Christians the other six days of the week," my dad's rationale for not going to church
18. There are literally hundreds of answers we can use for not going to Church

So we must ask ourselves this question. Why do we need to go to Church? We go because it is God's will for us to attend Church and worship Him. Jesus didn't just come into our world to die on the cross, but he came to form the foundation of His Catholic Church in the world by teaching the Apostles and other disciples of God's love for the world. The Church now becomes the vehicle for reaching out into the world and sharing with the people the Good News that Jesus offers the world, and sharing those Sacraments that bring grace into our lives of faith.

As a people, we are often messy and a creature of habits, many of us are also set in our ways in the way we look at the world. Remember my description of my siblings and how so very different we are in the ways we see and act in the world; even though we are so different in some areas of our lives—it is our love for each other that binds us together as a family. Our church is filled with folks who too have lived out their lives in a certain way. Each church brings together a wide variety of people with hundreds of differences, but we come together at Mass for a common purpose, and that is worshiping and honoring our God.

In an ideal world all members of Congress would live by the ideal that they are working for the welfare of every person within the country, so even with opposing views as to how to properly run the government—each man or woman in Congress would work through and fashion a bill that benefits the people of our country, with each side giving up certain areas of the bill they would have liked to see in the bill, in order to reach a consensus that would allow the bill to be passed into law, a law that could now benefit the most people. In the movie "Lincoln" I was reminded of the divisive nature of government and the verbal battles and the arm twisting that must occur to get a law passed, it was not a pretty process to watch.

In a smaller way there are similar differences being worked out within Church, it is one of the reasons why the Catholic Church has today 300 different ways they are called to worship as a Catholic and why there are 30,000 different Protestant denominations. We can all agree that Jesus is the head of the Mystical Body of Christ in our world today, a body that is made up of over seven billion people today. The world doesn't have 30,300 different Christian Mystical Bodies of Christ—there can only be one Body of Christ because Jesus died for all the people of the world, not just those who call themselves Christian, but all the people of the world.

Our vision of the world is small compared to God's vision; at the most we might know three or four hundred people in our little world, while God knows over seven billion people at their deepest levels of thought—because it was God who created them in the first place. Each one of us has been on earth for a relatively short period of time, while God has always existed. We must trust in God's plan for His world and accept His will over our lives. Don't worry about the differences between people—it is these differences that force us to work together for a common cause that unites us into a people of God. The world would be very boring if everybody thought and believed just like we did—we would all be asleep and bored out of our minds. No, it is those differences between people that adds color and passion to the world, the differences don't have to separate us, but they can propel us to deeper levels of faith and understanding of God, and a deeper level of love for another. The Mass is a natural model for us to use to shape how we are called to serve and worship God and our Lord Jesus each day. Here are the parts of the Daily Mass and the attitudes we must learn to follow in worshipping our God:

1. Bowing before the Lord (reverence towards God, recognizing God's place in the world)
2. Listening to God before Mass (kneeling before God, is a sign of great reverence and understanding of our role in this relationship with God)
3. Saying our prayers while kneeling (sign of reverence, our prayers will either honor God through our praise, or prayers of petition—where we are asking God for some grace to help us in life, Praying the rosary is really a short journey through the life of Christ—a beautiful set of prayers that helps keep us focused on everything Jesus has done for us and the world)
4. Entrance Procession: Standing up as a family, singing a song of welcome for God's presence in our lives (standing, a sign that we are ready to accept Jesus into our lives at Mass)
5. Greeting: Acknowledging the Lord before all the people (standing, a sign that we are ready to accept Jesus into our lives at Mass)
6. Penitential Rite: saying a prayer asking for forgiveness from our sins (standing, another prayer where we ask God for forgiveness from our sins and our short comings)
7. Kyrie: asking the Lord for mercy (Prayer of petition, asking God for grace)
8. Gloria: a prayer of praise and thanksgiving (Prayer of praise and thanksgiving)
9. Opening Prayer: (Priests blesses us with a prayer from the Lord)

10. Liturgy of the Word: a time for listening to the words from holy scripture (sitting, a sign that demonstrates that we are being receptive to the Word of God)
    a. Reading from Old Testament
    b. Reading from the Psalms (this Psalm is often sung by the people)
    c. Reading from the Letters of the New Testament
    d. Reading from the Gospel (standing, a sign that we are eager to listen to and respond to the Good News of the Gospel)
11. Homily: Priest shares his thoughts and teachings on the scriptures being read today (sitting down, means that we are receptive to the teaching found in the four readings of scripture)
12. Profession of Faith, proclaiming the Apostle's Creed (standing up, a sign that tells we are ready to proclaim and believe in the truths found in the Apostle's Creed)
13. Intercessions: praying for the needs of the people and world (standing before God and asking help for the needs of our family, parish and world)
14. Collection of tithes (sitting down, giving our tithes and energies for the needs of the church)
15. Liturgy of the Eucharist
    a. Presentation of gifts (standing, prayer for giving ourselves to Jesus, the gifts and abilities we were born with, along with our tithe offerings—as a way to honor God for His many gifts of grace and mercy)
    b. Prayer over the gifts of the people (standing, the priest prays to God and thanks God for these gifts, gifts that can now be used for the building up of his church)
    c. Eucharistic prayer (kneeling, a sign that recognizes that we are reliving the Last Supper with Jesus, a time for preparing our hearts for receiving the Body and Blood of Christ, a very holy moment in the Mass)

    d. Memorial acclamation (standing up and proclaiming the Great Amen to the world, I believe in your words and truth for my life Jesus—a truth that in a few moments will be consumed by us at communion)

16. Communion Rite

    a. The Lord's prayer (standing, sharing a communal prayer of the prayer the Lord Jesus taught his Apostles)

    b. Sign of Peace between people (standing, shaking/ hugging your neighbors in the pews)

    c. Breaking the bread (Priest says some prayers over the Eucharist and wine)

    d. Communion: Lamb of God (standing, another prayer that prepares our heart and soul for communion)

    e. Communion: Receiving the Body and Blood of Jesus Christ(walking towards the altar where we receive Christ into our body, we say Amen, a sign that says we believe that this is the Risen Jesus we are consuming at communion)

    f. Communion song of thanks (kneeling or sitting, singing a song of thanksgiving for what we just received from Jesus)

    g. Period of silence (a silent prayer or reflection about what Jesus gave to us in the various parts of the Mass, the day's scripture reading, the songs sang that day, or from what we received from Jesus at Communion)

    h. Prayer after communion

17. Concluding Rite: (sending the people off with a blessing (standing, ready to put our faith in action in the world we live)

18. Closing song (sending the people off with a song (standing, ready to put our faith in action)

As a child we had the opportunity for going on vacation with our parents out west, we usually travelled to visit our great aunts Blanche and Edith out in the Los Angeles area. And on these trips west we were often given a chance to buy one or two souvenirs, and the one souvenir that always caught my eyes were those rocks that were polished and smoothed down. Even today I still keep several smooth rocks on my bookcase—I am drawn to them each day as I pass my bookcase.

In many ways when we first attend church we are like those rocks inside the tumbler, our edges are rough because of our personality and what we have learned from the world. Inside a church community over time those hard edges of our personality are broken down to where they are polished and smooth to the touch. If we looked at the other stones in the tumbler there will be many others that survived and were made beautiful as well. But, we also know that there are some rocks for whatever reason crumble down to sand. I think with the rocks that survived it required a level of faith as the Lord broke down the hard edges off our lives. I have known people who couldn't take the tension found within a community—and so they either turn inward and away from God, or they choose to worship God in their own way at home.

Our journey in Following Jesus on the Narrow Path to God is a singular journey because we have only one soul within our body, but that Narrow Path we are following is the exact same Narrow Path that every other person in the world must follow. It doesn't mean we are "alone" on this journey, for Jesus guides us along the path through his love and will for our lives. It is with the direction and love of our faith community which gives us an added strength to stay on the narrow path. Here a a few examples again:

1. Holy Spirit will always take us to Jesus, and He will convict us of our sins—so we can forever leave them at the foot of the cross.
2. The Church founded by Jesus will show us the way to Jesus
   a. The Word of God takes us to Jesus

    b. The Sacraments takes us to Jesus
3. The Master teachers show us the way to Jesus
    a. Virgin Mary
    b. Saints
    c. Bishops
    d. God's special people
4. The Disciples will show us the way to Jesus
    a. Priests and ministers
    b. Godly parents / siblings / relatives
    c. Godly friends

Who am I?

1. I am a husband and father
2. I am twenty to thirty years old
3. I spend twelve to sixteen hours a day at work, my arms and legs are strong and calloused, my face is rugged because of all the harsh weather I have to endure each day. I work alongside and lead three or four other guys who must complete the tasks I assign them at a moment's notice—otherwise we might not earn the money needed to provide for our family's needs
4. I am an average guy who attends church on Saturday, I am a man who loves and adores my wife and children. I have been known to have a "good" time with my friends as well.

Have you figured out who I am yet? I could be any one adult throughout history—even you!

5. I am a fisherman in the Sea of Galilee

That's right I am Peter, a man that God had picked and prepared for His son's famous question. Will you join my path and follow me, and if you do I will make you a fisher of men?

We know that Peter took that first step following Jesus on the narrow path, but it was only a step in the right direction and nothing else. Peter didn't become the Head of the Church that Jesus was preparing with his first step. No, but Peter and the other Apostles and disciples were given the grace by God to follow Jesus during those two/three years of the Lord's ministry:

1. They witnessed to the Lord's every teaching on God
2. They witnessed the Lord's teaching to the common every day folk about God
3. They witnessed Jesus healing many people
4. They witnessed how Jesus prayed to God and they were taught a prayer by Jesus
5. They witnessed firsthand the Word of God being spoken to them
6. They witnessed the magnitude of the Lord's love for people
7. They learned firsthand how to align their will with Jesus, for this was exactly how Jesus lived his life in serving God's will, a will that even placed him on a cross carrying each of our sins.

Peter was just like anyone else in the world, we do the tasks that we need to complete each day, in order to earn money that can be used to provide for our family's physical needs, and we make the effort in providing a sense of our love to each of our family. But, Peter was asked by Jesus to join him on this journey of faith. Peter did the work that was required of him—he listened to the Lord's teachings and struggled to understand what they meant first for their own lives and then for what these teachings meant for the rest of the world. Peter witnessed the many healings God worked through Jesus—again there was a feeling of wonder for these miracles from God and a level of confusion as to how Jesus was able to heal people. Both Peter and the other Apostles were given opportunities for putting their faith into practice: preaching God's love and truth from the words Jesus gave them, healing the people with the power that Jesus gave them, sending away demons and evil spirits from the people who were possessed—with the power and conviction that Jesus gave them. Peter started off as just a man, when he stepped on the narrow path he became a disciple and follower of Christ, in time with knowledge and practice in doing God's will, Peter now had the skills and abilities needed by an Apostle. Mary was a simple holy child of God who becomes the vessel in which the Son of God was able to enter the world. Jean Vianney was a son of a farmer in some obscure corner of France, a man who accepted the call from Jesus to become a Priest, and Jean did the work needed in learning about the ways and truths of God from the books he studied, and the hours he spent in prayer with Jesus. Jean worked twenty hours a day serving the needs of the Lord: in saying Mass, in his daily prayers, in begging for money for rebuilding the church, in gathering rocks for the church, in visiting the people in the area of Ars, and in spending at least fifteen hours a day in the confessional. Much of the people of France were brought back to God because Jesus worked this one simple son of a farmer who became a priest.

Accept God's call for following Jesus on the Narrow Path, it will be the most important step of your life, and it will be a step you will never regret for you will see how the whole world will open up before you, a world of great beauty for it is complete and perfect in God's eyes. But as long as we can still see the pain and anguish of the world then we must also know that we will be asked by Jesus to help him heal our broken world, and to restore all peoples back to His Father in Heaven.

Remember what the Cure of Ars told the people of his parish about heaven *"But it is not difficult to get to heaven? No my friends, you can go to heaven by keeping a simple little rule. Do only those things that are pleasing to God!"*[109]

---

[109]   *p. 28, excerpt used from "The Cure of Ars: The Priest Who Out-Talked the Devil," by Milton Lomask, Ignatius Press, 1958, used with permission, (http://www.ignatius.com)*